GOBIERNO DEL ESTADO
LIBRE Y SOBERANO
DE BAJA CALIFORNIA

DEPENDENCIA	STATE SECRETARY OF TOURISM OF BAJA CALIFORNIA
SECCION	TIJUANA
NUMERO DEL OFICIO	
EXPEDIENTE	T/01/109/88

ASUNTO: WELCOME

Tijuana, B.C. March 25th. 1988.

Dear Friends:

Bonnie Wong's **Bicycling Baja** opens a new door to unique rewarding, and memorable firsthand experiences with the people of our land.
We especially commend her encouragement to use the safety and support
network of rural ranchos which complement the full services available
in the towns of our magnificent peninsula. Travelers always benefit
from the increased peace of mind that comes from knowing that assistance is close at hand, should it be needed.
The identification of these support services, coupled with
the most detailed and accurate route descriptions available anywhere,
make this guide invaluable for all Baja travelers. Motorcyclist,
off road enthusiast, nature lore and history buffs, equestrians, photo-
graphers, campers and armchair adventures too will more appreciate
the beauty and warmth of the great natural and human resources of
Baja California.
From Tijuana, North America's second largest west coast city,
to land's end a thousand miles away at Cabo San Lucas, this book
promotes goodwill and enhances carefree travel in our friendly country.
The highways and byways of Baja become magic pathways to mutual understanding and enjoyment for tourist and resident alike. The memories
of special moments or days will last forever, transcending the narrow
bounds of time and nationality, to the farther horizons of fun, fellow-
ship and sharing our common dreams on our very uncommon planet.
Bienvenidos, welcome, to the land and people of the sun.

Sincerely,

JOSE LUIS RENDON B.
SECRETARY OF TOURISM
BAJA CALIFORNIA, MEXICO.

SECRETARIA DE
TURISMO DEL ESTADO
DESPACHADO
MAR 25 1968
DESPACHADO
TIJUANA, B. C.

MORE REVIEW COMMENTS

An informative, detailed and clearly written guide.... Wong provides complete information...that will apply to every touring cyclist (and touring drivers, as well).... I wouldn't bike in Baja without it.
---**San Diego Union**

The book is a big help for the adventure minded mountain biker.
---**Mountain Bike Action Magazine**

Excellent road logs! Easy reading and very informative. Bonnie Wong's attentiveness to detail give readers everything they need for an enjoyable bicycling experience in Baja.
---**Mexico West Travel Club, Inc.**

An excellent guide...here is the book that has long been needed.
---**La Siesta Press** (publisher of **Baja Road Log, Camping and Climbing in Baja**, and **Beaches of Baja**)

The mileage logs detail every turn in the road giving a good idea of what to expect up ahead.... BICYCLING BAJA is well-written book by someone who's bicycled Baja again and again.
---**Bicycling San Diego Magazine**

It is an easy to read book.... Even the non-cyclist Baja enthusiast will find the book entertaining (and informative) reading.... BICYCLING BAJA provides essential information for the biker. We recommend the guide as *must reading*!
---**Baja Times**

BICYCLING
BAJA

AMIGOS

Amigos
come with me!
Come cleanse your souls!

Where shall we go?

There where the desert lures,
where winds play sweetest songs
on cactus' thorn,
where silent road is dreaming
and waits for those of purest heart.

Where shall we take our rest?
Under the distant stars
on earth's warm breast.

What shall we see?
What shall we hear?

Far away mountains
where lonely vultures are slowly circling
death and life.

The vast horizons
singing sea
dark children's laughter
where echoing sky meets soul
in healing silence.

Come,
amigos
come with me!

Marie Danes, "Baja Lovers," 1979

BICYCLING BAJA

Cyclists' Guide to Major Scenic and Historic Routes Through Fabulous Baja California

by BONNIE WONG

Sunbelt Publications
San Diego

Sunbelt Publications
POB 191126
San Diego, CA 92119-1126   All inquiries should be accompanied by a
self-addressed, stamped envelope.

Library of Congress Cataloging-in-Publication Data

Wong, Bonnie, 1946
    Bicycling Baja : cyclists' guide to major scenic and historic
routes through fabulous Baja California / by Bonnie Wong. -- 1st ed.
    p.   cm.
    Bibliography: p.
    Includes index.
    ISBN 0-932653-04-9 : $12.95 (est.)
    1. Bicycle touring--Mexico--Baja California--Guide-books. 2. Baja
California (Mexico)--Description and travel--Guide-books.
I. Title.
GV1046.M6W66 1988
917.2'2--dc19   88-2371
                                                                         CIP

First Edition
1 2 3 4 5 6 7 8 9 10

TO

Those who have that

special Baja spirit

ACKNOWLEDGEMENTS

Over the years my riding companions on the Baja roads have been many and varied. Our explorations were always unpredictable, funny, frustrating, adventuresome and ultimately memorable. I thank all those riders, especially those of the 1970s when Baja bicycle touring was in its infancy, who trusted me when I said we'd have fun!

Two companions in particular stand out as having made many such spirited trips, Claire Harvey during the 1970s, and Mari Friend in the 1980s, were always ready to go Baja adventuring. I thank them for their sharing; these were always journeys with a difference.

In preparation of this book, I want to thank Sunbelt Publications editor, Bill Hample, and publishers, Diana and Lowell Lindsay, for their enthusiasm, encouragement and great assistance. Vital proofing was supplied by Armando Carrasco of the Baja State Department of Tourism and by Dave Dickson of Bicycling West. The presentation of the routes is greatly enhanced by the excellent maps prepared by Kathy Steffen, also a Baja Biker, and by Bill Hample. I'd also like to thank my husband, Wade, for all the dinners he prepared during the spring of 1987 when I forgot what time it was.

Bonnie Wong
Port Townsend, WA
1988

CONTENTS

Mari Friend on road between sister villages of San Isidro and La Purisima

INTRODUCTION

Every winter since 1973 I have returned to Baja and every winter, tour companions and I face a litany of negative, stereotyped reasons why we shouldn't go to Mexico, from well-meaning friends.

My greatest satisfaction has been to see these unfair images dissolve. Cyclists' attitudes toward the Mexicans as people and Baja as a special environment have been transformed into something positive. As a group leader, I have merely provided the opportunity. The trip itself has been the catalyst of the process - a small contribution to international understanding.

This guide won't answer all your questions nor would I want it to. Part of the fun of a bicycle tour is exploring and discovery. For instance, I left out my "bakery treasure maps" on purpose - seeking out good bakeries is well worth the time! Many cyclists have now toured Baja and whatever their personal reactions, all agree - Baja is one of a kind!

Every effort has been made to make the information presented herein accurate and current. Baja, however, is not static and is in a constant state of change. Just because a rancho was open and serving delicious meals at reasonable prices yesterday doesn't mean it will do so tomorrow. My opinions have been formed by several years of experience and may seem off-base at first. What I say about Baja may not apply to all of Mexico. My favorite quote about Baja is from Bob Wagner: "In Baja, remain rigidly flexible."

I have found cycling in Baja to be an excellent way to experience a close by and very special part of the world. I hope this book will help you come to a similar conclusion.

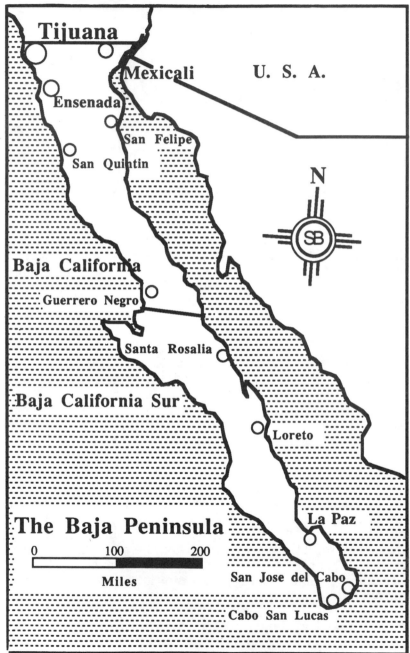

The Baja Peninsula

1

BAJA BACKGROUND

About This Book

This book was designed to provide bicyclists with a variety of tours - long, short, difficult, easy - by which they might experience the fun and adventure of cycling in a different world. This is a world where the language is different, as are the money, food, customs and the land itself. This world is Baja California and Baja California Sur, two states in a foreign country, yet so close to home that excellent one or two day bike tours out of San Diego are possible. The book describes:

1.   Five short tours just across the U. S. Border. See "Day Rides Near the Border." These tours may be combined to form longer rides if desired.

2.   Seven tours which may be taken individually, in combinations, or as one long chain down the full length of the Baja peninsula from Tijuana to Cabo San Lucas. Public transportation to the point(s) of entry of each tour or tour combination, is described. See "Transpeninsular Tours."

3.   Four mountain bike   tours   for those who enjoy a challenge as well as the rugged, back-country environment. See "Rough Stuff (Mountain Bike) Tours."

4.   The logistics or "The How" of preparing for a Baja bicycle tour - such things as equipment needed, paperwork, tips on food, camping, etc. See "Logistics."

Included as Appendices are the usual Baja compilation of Spanish terms and their English counterparts, a narrative description of an actual Baja mountain bike tour over the famous Baja 1000 route, maps, lists of pertinent publications, etc.

Finally, whether it be bicycling, hiking, scuba diving, swimming, or any number of other outdoor activities, the buddy system, i.e. "never-go-it-alone," is recognized as the safest way to go. When biking in Baja the buddy system is strongly recommended. However, what usually happens is that the original buddies develop into a group, and with proper planning, a group tour of Baja can be a highly enjoyable experience. Should you become the leader of such an endeavor (and if the tour was your idea in the first place, you more than likely will), see   the Appendix "Considerations for Potential Group Leaders and Others."

If after reading this book you would like to see Baja but still have your doubts, I would suggest you try one of the annual fun rides which are offered. Or, if you would like to go even further before going it on your own, try one of the commercially conducted tours. Listings of the major annual rides and commercially conducted biking tours are included as Appendices.

The Land

Baja California is essentially a peninsula stretching in a southeasterly direction some 800 miles from the international border at San Diego. It varies in width from about 30 to 145 miles, is bounded on the east by the Colorado River and the Gulf of California (Sea of Cortez), and on the west by the Pacific Ocean. A single line of mountain ranges runs the general length of the peninsula. As with the Sierra Nevada range in California, the mountains rise gradually on their western sides and fall off sharply on the east. The highest peak is Picacho del Diablo (10,123 feet) west of San Felipe. The general altitudes of the peninsula tend to decrease from north to south. The eastern side of Baja is dry and desert-like, little or no surf conditions exist along its beaches, and temperatures become very high in summer. The western side of Baja sees heavy surf due to the Pacific swell, sea breezes and coastal fog similar to Southern California are experienced, while many of the flatter areas are desert-like.

The peninsula is divided into two Mexican states: Baja California to the north and Baja California Sur to the south. Their common border is the 28th parallel. The parallel is also the border between the Pacific and Mountain Time Zones.

Migrino Beach, north of Cabo San Lucas on Pacific side

The Climate

The climate along the Pacific coast of Baja California is similar to that of across-the-border Southern California. Rainfall decreases to the south but picks up again in the Cabo San Lucas region due to tropical storms. The average rainfall at Ensenada is about 10 inches per year, south at Bahia Magdalena about 4 inches per year, and at Cabo San Lucas about 9 inches per year.

November through April can be very pleasant. December and January are the coolest months and can be cold at night in the northern half. Along the Sea of Cortez it is generally 10 to 15 degrees warmer, while summer temperatures can soar to 110 degrees F., accompanied by relatively high humidity. However, the humidity is not as high as on the Mexican mainland. The tropical area south of La Paz has occasionally experienced late summer tropical hurricanes. However, more frequently heavy squalls, called *chubascos*, occur.

History - The Missions

Most of Baja's early history is obscure and centers around five Indian groups on the peninsula. Very little is known about them. The Spanish explorers made several futile attempts at colonizing the peninsula in the early 1500s. It was the Roman Catholic missionary movement which was eventually successful at forcing the land and people of Baja to succumb to the white man's presence on a permanent basis.

1533   An expedition by Fortin Jimenez from mainland Mexico landed in what is now called La Paz Bay. The contingent was almost wiped out by the Indians.

1535   Hernando Cortez reentered the area in search of a rumored bounty of pearls. Settlement again failed and the inhospitable peninsula was left unexplored for the next 150 years.

1683 A young Jesuit named Francisco Kino made another settlement attempt at La Paz. It too failed.

1697 Another Jesuit, Juan Salvatierra, founded the first successful mission in Baja California at Loreto. This started the Jesuit period lasting 71 years. Twenty missions were founded on the peninsula, thus establishing a powerful influence over the destiny of Baja.

1767 Through political forces in Europe the Jesuits were expelled from all Spanish dominions, including Baja. Only about half of their 20 missions were considered successful. Between 1742 and 1748, disease epidemics devastated the mission converts.

1768 The Franciscan order replaced the Jesuits and immediately set up missions further north in San Diego and Monterey, with one mission north of Catavina in Baja. Northern Baja remained unexplored. When the Jesuits left Baja, the Dominican order also petitioned Spain for a place in Baja.

Mission at San Ignacio

1772   The Dominicans were allowed to take over the old Jesuit missions in Baja and extend north to meet the Fran-
ciscans' efforts. The Dominicans established 9 new
missions as far north as San Diego. Together the Fran-
ciscans and Dominicans were active on the peninsula
some 53 years and added 10 missions to the system.

By now the mission populations had been ravaged by venereal
and other contagious diseases to the point where there were
few souls to save and few left to work the missions. It is
estimated 50,000 to 70,000 Indians were on the peninsula
when the movement began. This dwindled to 5,000 by the
close of the movement. By 1821 and the revolution which
ensued, the mission system in Baja was all but abandoned.
With a short-lived gold discovery in 1848, many settlers from
the mainland made their way to the peninsula and a new era of
exploration began. By and large, however, Baja became the
forgotten peninsula far removed from mainland Mexico.

The People

Baja's population is concentrated along the U.S. border in the
north and in the La Paz - Cabo San Lucas area to the south.
The in-between is sparsely settled and its towns are relatively
small. Tijuana, Ensenada and Mexicali are the hubs of trade,
agriculture and industrialized growth. Agricultural development is spreading south from the border while tourism is
bringing growth to the San Jose del Cabo region.

Mexico is considered a third-world country. It has
experienced rapid industrial growth, however, and is now
classified by the World Bank as a Middle Income Developing
Country. As in so many developing countries, much of this
growth has been accomplished by a socialistic approach. The
CONASUPO stores, gasoline (PEMEX), the FONATUR
tourist developments, the fishing industry, airlines, banks,
etc., are government controlled. Evidences of improvements
sponsored by the government are seen throughout Baja.

While the lot of the average Baja Californian has improved, the people, for the most part, have retained their patient, friendly attitude toward visitors. It is true that "jerks" are not restricted to any single nationality or ethnic group, and Baja has its share. But so has that other vast area of North America which lies north of the U.S. - Mexico border. I have found that in most cases where the "Ugly American" image is not exhibited, friendly and harmonious relations with Baja Californians usually result.

Official Assistance

The most knowledgable and helpful agency for travelers in Baja is the State Department of Tourism. It is available for assistance in planning a tour. The address is:

>Baja State Department of Tourism
>P.O. Box 2448
>Chula Vista, CA 92012

The telephone numbers of the various Baja State Tourism Offices are:

>(706) 681-9492, 9493, or 9494 (in Tijuana)
>(706) 654-1095 Tecate
>(706) 676-2222 Ensenada
>(706) 552-4391 Mexicali
>(706) 577-1155 San Felipe

The public assistance personnel in this department are most cordial, very fluent in English, and are generous with factual advice on matters of greatest concern to travelers. A pre-trip telephone call or visit can be most helpful for such questions as road conditions, accomodations, specifics of Mexican law, regulations, insurance, and the judicial system.

2

LOGISTICS

Getting Started

If by chance you mention to a non-biker (or even some bikers) that you are planning a bicycle trip into Mexico, be prepared! A litany of impending "horrors" will be repeated over and over. Because I've been to Baja before, the negatives are usually presented as questions. For a first-timer expect statements of absolute fact even if, as is the usual case, your lecturer has never been to Mexico. The universal topics covered are: bad people (*bandidos*), bad water, food and *turista*, Montezuma's Revenge, or just plain violent diarrhea. Further, he will go on, everyone knows what bad drivers Mexicans are. The conclusion is obvious.   You're crazy to take a trip to Baja! And so it goes.

If, at this point, you are still with us, GREAT! Getting started is perhaps the toughest part. Once the commitment is made plans usually fall quickly into place.   I have entitled this chapter "Logistics." While it doesn't cover fully the military definition, i.e.,"The procurement, maintenance, and transportation of materiel, facilities, and personnel," some of the items mentioned herein do fall into these categories and should most certainly be included in your plans.

If the spirit is willing, but you still have some doubts, then before lining up your buddies for your own safari, try, as I have suggested, one of the annual cycling events or fun rides into Baja (see Appendix). Some of the biggest boosts toward promoting cycling south of the border are these annual fun ride cycling events.   There are also the commercial bike tours (also listed in the Appendix). Whatever your persuasion, after getting your feet wet, so to speak, commitment to an all-out tour of your own may come easier. But if you're mentally ready to get there, and read this guide to work out a few logistics, then I suggest you make your own judgment - go and try it!

Spring wildflowers and Mari Friend near Laguna Hanson

Accommodations and Camping

Accommodations

During my tours into Baja, we have occasionally stayed in RV parks and motels. In the tour listings (see Chapter 3, "The Tours") I have noted the locations of some motels and RV parks. Be advised that motel and other commercial accommodations in Baja do not always meet north-of-the-border standards. However, some of the newest and finest Mexican luxury-resort hotels are found on the southern end of the peninsula (bring your credit card!). If you are planning to spend some or all of your nights in motel, hotel, or other commercial accommodations, I suggest you obtain an accommodation directory for guidance. The Automobile Club of Southern California (AAA) publishes a very good one, "Baja California Accommodations." However, at this time it is not really possible to make a long, all-motel tour unless you are able to do 135 miles in a day.

Camping

The complete freedom of when and where to camp each night has been one of the most satisfying highlights of the Baja tour for me. Because of the unrestricted camping opportunities, one can easily travel "at his own pace" in the truest sense. To travel with an unstructured itinerary is a romantic notion not many tourists have the chance to pursue. In Baja, it can be done!

Bonafide campground facilities are still few and far between; yet services are becoming more available at important road junctions. You are still welcome to simply pull off the road at day's end and select your own space.

Wonderful camping options still abound throughout the peninsula, but, since the early 1980s, greater development of agriculture and grazing in the far north and tourism in the Cape region have brought on more and more fences. In the case of grazing, the fences are not meant to keep you out, but to keep the livestock in. There is a significant toll of animals hit by vehicles. One reason there is such a big warning about not driving at night is because the animals sleep on the warm roadway after sundown. In the case of the Cape region, most of the fences you will find are on the beach side of the road. These areas are being developed at a rapid rate, yet many spots are still public beaches - *playas de publico*. There are often openings in the fences adequate to get a bicycle through, but not a vehicle. So much the better, at least for the time being. It will change. Using the road log in these sections, to find the side roads, will greatly help you plan your daily distance.

Primitive camping has its special rewards for those willing to carry along their own water, tablecloth and toilet paper. Finding a deserted beach to camp on, from the paved road, is getting harder to do with the influx of RVs and 4-wheel drives; but, finding clean, empty and quiet pieces of desert is easy. Whether camping in the desert or along the beautiful beaches, the escapade will be exactly what you make of it. If you enjoy nature in its wilderness state, I don't think you'll be disappointed. The tranquil purity is hard to beat. I find many cycle tourists are afraid of the desert and quite apprehensive about just stopping "in the middle of nowhere." That has become part of the joy of the group tours, watching people make the transition from fenced-in cubicles and the normal amenities to the natural environment as the preferred environment.

People traveling with me quickly learn my peculiarities in selecting a campsite. These are some of the considerations:

1.   Use a side road off the highway to get some distance from the traffic and to avoid traversing through thorns.

2.   Avoid tops and bottoms of hills (Mexican vehicles seldom have mufflers and are very noisy).

3.   If windy, find a leeward side of rocks or hills.

4.   Once down a side road there will be little if any traffic, so carry bikes a short distance to the side to avoid cactus punctures.

5.   Avoid camping near a rancho or town - burros, cows, dogs and roosters seem to make noise all night (coyotes do, too, but are part of the "experience").

6.   Stay out of those nice, soft, sandy arroyos.   Flash floods are not to be fooled with.

7.   Avoid putting a tent on an animal trail - those trails are often used at night!

Once your spot is chosen, you will find ample dead cactus wood for a pleasant campfire.   Even dead wood still has thorns.   Kick, or shake, wood before picking up and carry pieces away from your body.   You may be disturbing the home of small scorpions which are often seen scampering out of the fire-ring.   These are small, 1" to 1-1/2" long, salmon colored and are non-fatal to adults, but have a painful sting.

You will need to spend a little time carefully cleaning an area of thorns and little stones on which to erect your tent.   For a tent, I would suggest one with a floor, mosquito netting and a rain-fly.   The floor and netting are good because of possible scorpions, tarantulas or snakes - with none of which we've ever had a problem.   A rain-fly is good because the desert loves to dew.   Dew and fog moisture are much more prevalent on the Pacific side.   Free standing tents have an advantage for sandy beach camping, though nothing beats just sleeping out in the sand for me.

A lightweight ground cloth (piece of rip stop nylon does fine) helps save the tent floor and is handy to pull out for those noon-time siestas.

The desert floor is hard ground indeed and a good insulated sleeping pad is desirable, as the earth becomes quite cold at night.

If the joy of primitive camping is the lure of a pristine environment, then it follows that the camper has an obligation to preserve such an environment.   No-impact camping is nothing new, but is even more imperative in the desert where disintegration of litter and wastes takes many times longer than in other areas.   Finding a clean spot means leaving it clean. Dig a fire pit and cover it over in the morning.   Do the same for human wastes and burn the toilet paper.   Lightweight plastic garden trowels work fine for these duties.

If the idea of just pulling off the road anywhere you feel like it doesn't appeal to your sense of adventure, then simply ask permission to camp next to a rancho.   The people will be more than glad to let you sleep on their property.   They think it inconceivable that you would want to sleep in the desert!

WATER, FOOD AND HEALTH

Water

Realizing that towns with water are farther apart than a day's ride for many cycle tourists, the obvious question is, "Where do you get water?" The availability of water on most U.S. tours is taken for granted, but is of real concern when touring in Baja.

Without doubt, water is a very heavy item for the cyclist to carry and one of several psychological hurdles people have to accept as part of the Baja tour. Risking a case of dehydration for the sake of a lighter bike just isn't worth it. Besides, with adequate water on board, your day can remain unrushed and camp can be made wherever it looks good.

How much you need is dependent upon the weather, how far to the next source, and what kind of cooking you plan to do. Along the paved roads, water can be supplemented with frequent stops at ranchos for beer or pop, both of which are usually available.

Most towns along Highway 1 will sell bottled water in 1 gallon plastic containers at the local *abarrotes* or *conasupo*. This isn't always the case at smaller *ejido* stores. Likewise, towns with stores big enough to sell water also have "city" water available. The public water system is safe to drink from and easy to find. You can find a faucet at the plaza (in towns big enough to have plazas), sometimes located under benches or in bushes. Otherwise, ask where to get "*agua potable.*" The locals will let you know where it's good and where it's not.

The long stretch between El Rosario and Guerrero Negro (221 miles) leaves you dependent upon the ranchos to replenish your water supply. Ranchos (roadside farmhouses) with a well (some have windmills easily spotted from the road) are a good source of drinking water. Be observant, however, as to the source of rancho water as many do not have wells. These get their water from a delivery truck and store it in 50 gallon drums. If you do take this water, purify it or use it for cooking.

Another source of water is from the frequent RVs passing by. Those traveling south undoubtedly have U. S. water while those going north have obtained it from a good source.

Because there is no steady stream of ranchos in the backcountry to supplement your diet with sodas and beer, even more water has to be carried. This, of course, depends on what particular route is chosen and how many ranchos are along the way. Meals that don't require a lot of water to prepare should be a consideration.

Food

Tourista, the Mexican "two-step", or "Montezuma's Revenge" are well-known facets of travel south of the border. Bicycling with the "two-step" would be miserable, to say the least.

I have no magic formula for keeping people healthy nor any explanation as to why someone in a group gets sick when we all eat and drink the same food and water at the same places. Getting sick is the exception rather than the rule, as most groups go the entire tour without someone contracting the "two-step."

The biggest difference between touring Baja now and in the 1970s, as far as food is concerned, is refrigeration. On my first long tour of the peninsula, we ate eggs and beans at the ranchos the entire trip with only an occasional piece of fish. Except in the largest towns, meat just wasn't offered unless you hit it lucky. Not only is beer cold now, but meat and dairy products are available at most stores and even ranchos. When eating out now, pork, *machaca*, meat *burritos*, fish, *chorizo*, beef steak or chicken may be offered. Another big change is that all meals were served with beans and rice. Now, french fries and beans are much more common. Potatoes have arrived in Baja. The milk is pasturized and fine to drink.

Sometimes yogurt and cheeses from the U. S. are available but expensive. Local cheeses range from salty goats milk cheese to the excellent and expensive cheese from mainland Mexico.

Obviously, products from the U. S. or fruit from mainland Mexico will be more expensive than Baja produced products. By and large, food in Baja is a little more expensive than similar food in mainland Mexico.

You have to approach grocery shopping with a wait-and-see attitude. Walking in with a preconceived menu and shopping list can lead to disappointment. If you're not in a huge rush and there are more than one or two stores, check them out on a trial run. It's not unusual to find completely different lines of food between them. One may have lots of vegetables while the other has a good selection of canned goods, or perhaps meat.

Pastas, canned vegetables and canned meats (tuna, sardines), crackers and cookies are almost always available at the smallest *abarrotes*. When the pickings are slim, it's nice to have a small assortment of spices in the kitchen kit to add some interest to the recipe.

The general rule I've personally used when eating in Mexico is to stick with cooked foods or those that can be peeled. There are on-going arguments about the types of fertilizers being used and this eating routine reduces the odds. With access to more and more water, the northern fields of Baja are quickly becoming a "bread basket" for markets elsewhere, including the U. S. Stringent import regulations, of course, have to be met, but those same regulations may not be used for the produce sold locally. I still stay away from lettuce and tomatoes while group members eat them on a daily basis with no ill effects. Work into the eating and drinking of local products slowly to let your system adjust and use common discretion and caution. If the water is something that really concerns you, then I say buy it and not spend your energy worrying about it. Enjoy the trip instead. I'd also advise you to use extreme caution if starting anti-diarrhea medication (tetracycline is one) prior to the trip.

There is so much hype about how cheap Mexico is. Because of the falling peso, people get the notion they can eat very well on a dollar a day. How soon they find out! Prices are lower than in the U. S. for comparable meals, but they aren't free. A reasonable budget is $5 - $7 a day if you include one meal a day at a rancho or cafe. Those meals typically run $2 to $3 plus the number of drinks you consume. It's not unusual for the pop or beer portion to be another dollar if it's hot. Interestingly enough, a meal of eggs and beans will cost about the same as a fish dinner at ranchos. In towns the cafes have actual menus and you can see the prices. From Santa Rosalia on south prices start to creep up. When you get to a tourist-oriented area the prices reflect what the market will bear. In

Brian Rovira fillets a fish for dinner

Cabo San Lucas you can expect to pay prices similar to home at the main restaurants. Inexpensive eating places are around. You have to look a little, and plan on eating with Spanish rather than English-speaking customers.

Eating is always a focus of any trip anywhere and this is certainly true in Baja. Ranchos become a highlight and certainly some offer exceptional bargains.

Health

Turista is the major concern of most potential cycle tourists. As already mentioned it is not as big a problem as it seems. You do not have to boil the water in Baja nor avoid the rancho food.

Sunburn is a more common problem within a group than *turista*. People coming south on a winter trip are often pale, having not seen the hot sun for a couple of months. A good sun block is essential and needs to be applied on Day One. A lightweight cotton, long-sleeved shirt is also recommended to cover up the arms after a couple of hours worth of sun.

Because people have such anxieties over the water, they tend to hoard or ration it. This quickly leads to dehydration, which in turn can manifest itself as heat exhaustion. Sunburn and dehydration are bad situations for the body, resulting in high temperatures, disorientation, inattention and weakness. The old adage about drinking before you are thirsty is imperative for desert travel. If making the effort to carry water, do yourself a favor and drink it!

There are always questions about snakes and critters that sting. The desert is indeed home to various snakes, tarantulas and scorpions, but the desert is a big place and any of these are very seldom seen, if at all. Our closest encounter came on a dirt backroad trip. On a downhill run a rider drove over a sidewinder before it had time to get out of the road. No harm was done to the snake as we looked at the wiggly tracks it left in the soft sand.

Although people worry about the creatures of the desert, it is the marine life which often causes problems. In the various groups I have led, three people have been stung by sting rays. These are often found along the shoreline in shallow water, just barely covered over with sand. The sharp sting is extremely painful. Once we were close enough to a town with a clinic where these sting cases were common. The situation was handled easily. Another time some Mexicans at the beach took over the situation with a bucket of boiled water. They submerged the foot in the bucket and massaged the foot in downward strokes. After about 30 minutes of this, the victim felt relief and was walking normally soon after.

Emergency

In the event of an accident, or emergency, there are some alternatives. There are a few doctors, modern clinics and hospitals along the peninsula. You can also get emergency medical treatment at a Red Cross (Cruz Roja) first aid station. Depending on the location and severity of your condition, you may want to return to the U.S. for treatment. A passing motorist, or bus going north, may be the quickest way. This is recommended only for minor injuries (e.g. broken arms) because the bus trip from La Paz (for example) takes about 26 hours and the trip would be even longer in a car or motorhome. At the border, medical emergencies can be handled, without waiting in line, by going to the closed gate at the left of the auto lines. A Customs Guard will arrive and let you through. The Binational Emergency Medical Care Committee at (619) 691-7000 may also assist in border crossing by arranging to send a land or air ambulance to pick you up, depending on your location in Baja.

Where immediate action is necessary, Air-Evac International, Inc. of San Diego (San Diego (619) 278-3822) can also help. Air-Evac will accept COLLECT calls from Baja. This is a completely equipped land/air ambulance service with a 24 hour dispatch center. With the call, arrangements must be made to cover costs before a flight can be made. Payment can be by major credit card or by a financial guarantee from a medical insurance company in the United States.

Preparations and Paperwork

You need one official paper to enter Baja south of Maneadero on Highway 1, or south of San Felipe on the dirt roads. The National Mexican Tourist offices located in major cities (See Appendix) throughout the U. S. and Canada offer these tourist cards or visas free. They are also available from Mexican Consulates, through your travel agent if you're flying in or out, Automobile Club of Southern California (AAA) offices or the Mexican immigration station at Maneadero. It is advisable to obtain your tourist card prior to crossing the border to avoid possible delays there.

Proof of citizenship is needed to get your tourist card and this identification should be carried with you during the trip. One of the following can be used: valid or expired passport, birth certificate, a notarized affidavit of nationality, or military I.D. that states U.S. nationality.

The tourist card needs to be validated after entering Mexico. There is a checkpoint at Maneadero for this purpose. If it is closed (if it is on Sunday) try La Pinta Hotel at Guerrero Negro or the ferry terminal at Santa Rosalia. If returning by land, no one makes an effort to collect these papers. If returning by air, they are collected and checked for validation. Over the years, I've been stopped on Highway 1 three times and asked to produce this document, so it is wise to be prepared.

A fishing license may be a worthwhile investment if you are so inclined. It is inexpensive and can be purchased at the Automobile Club of Southern California (AAA) by members, or in San Diego at: Mexico Department of Fisheries, 1010 2nd Ave. #1605. Call (619) 233-6956 for more information.

Another free document which may prove valuable is registration of foreign-made articles of value such as your bicycle and camera equipment if they are new. The customs office is located at 2262 Columbia St., San Diego, at most larger airports, or at the border. Should there ever be a question as to where you bought the items in question, this will avoid duty charges. Once you have the items declared, the form is good on any foreign trip you may take.

Mary Ann Bott   and small   friend at a rancho stop before La Paz, Highway 1

Equipment and Procedures

Bicycle Equipment

While the equipment descriptions which follow are applicable in their entirety to mountain bikes, many are also applicable to the standard touring bike. Your choice of equipment will depend upon your own preferences, which tours you plan to take and the types of roads and terrain that they include. However, the possibility of side excursions through rough and scenic country is ever-present in Baja and equipment should be chosen carefully with this in mind.

The following are my mountain bike equipment preferences and/or recommendations:

1.   Front and back racks are essential. They help distribute the load and with extra food and water carried, the space is needed. I recommend a regular platform-style front rack over the highly touted low-riders, which haven't worked well on rough, dirt roads. The platform also provides more space.

2.   I favor the heaviest possible knobby tires over the lightweight street tires, or combination tires. However, it really depends on how much of your tour is going to be on pavement. Do you want to lower your rolling resistance for pavement travel and sacrifice some handling ability on the dirt? That decision is up to you, although the route itself may determine which would be most appropriate. Some bikers go for lightweight tubes. I prefer the heavy duty ones and even use tire liners if not planning to take a spare tire. I hate flats on a loaded bike and the time and mess to change them. I am further willing to use heavier tires to keep pesky thorns at bay.

3.   I personally think fenders for a desert trip are a waste of time. Even with occasional water crossings, they are a nuisance most of the time. They are especially difficult to travel with if using public transportation.

4.   Pedals. - Some bikes come with bear-claw style pedals which can really "claw" your legs when walking a bike up or down a steep hill. The plastic ones seem to have a lower damage potential. This style, with a toe clip (strap optional), does a good job in keeping the foot in place during bumpy, or rocky, downhill descents. When coasting, exert a reasonable force on these pedals to keep your feet from jumping off same.

5.   Kickstand. - This accessory is shunned by most cyclists, but it is a real convenience on a mountain bike in Baja, or in other desert areas. There simply isn't anything to lean your bike against that is not armed with thorns. Laying the bike in the dirt isn't appealing either. There are currently some heavy duty models similar to the motor scooter type, which are installed on each side of the bike, making it virtually impossible for the bike to fall over.

6.   Cyclometer. - This is another essential accessory for back-country travel. In varied terrain, it is difficult to determine how fast, or slow, you are going. It is even more difficult to find road signs on back-country roads, much less road signs which show distances in miles or kilometers.

7.   Compass. - In addition to the aforementioned cyclometer for measuring distances, it is also important to know your direction of travel. True direction is not always obvious to the senses. Routes along the coasts are generally easy to follow because there are fewer roads running parallel. Furthermore, you always know where the water is. Once you are inland, there are often roads coming and going in every direction. These generally lead to someone's rancho and because the roads seem equally used, it is difficult to determine which is the "main" through road. A small compass is therefore a necessity.

8.   Topographic Maps. - These are another important aid to Baja back-country travel. Topo maps can be bulky to carry and expensive. The AAA map is quite accurate and does a fair job with dirt roads. It shows only the major roads in the back-country, however. Good topo maps show most roads and can be a real help in hill country. (See Appendix for sources).

Assorted equipment for self-contained dirt road trip

Camping Equipment

1.   I have used a one quart pot on a wood fire for cooking. Normally, however, I take along a stove. Mine happens to use white gas. I calculate a usage rate, then bring along enough white gas to last the whole tour. White gas is extremely difficult to find in Baja other than at Ciudad Constitucion and La Paz. Other Baja cyclists take a multi-fuel model and use EXTRA from the Pemex (nationalized Mexican gas station). EXTRA is the unleaded gasoline whereas NOVA is leaded. I use the Coleman simply because it works well for group cooking using big pots, allows simmering where required, and does not just act as a blow torch for boiling water.

2.   Sleeping Bag Liners. - These come in either cotton (heavy and bulky) or a very sheer, lightweight nylon. Because good thorough washing opportunities are infrequent in Baja, these liners help to keep your sleeping bag clean and free of body oils. They rinse quickly when opportunity allows. The sleeping bag liner can also be used on top of the bag during really hot nights. Liners may be purchased through local AYH Councils, or from the National Office, at a cost of about $15 (see Appendix for National Office address).

3.   Water Containers. - There are several water container options and frankly, I haven't found any of them to be 100% effective. For trips requiring a large capacity water container, I have taken a couple of the Water Sacs sold at sporting goods stores. They have a heavy plastic liner covered with a nylon material and have a handle for hanging the bag. The handle is an excellent idea, but in the thorn-infested desert, finding a safe hanging place can become a problem. If using a Water Sac, carry along an extra bladder (this can be obtained from wine and apple juice boxes) and an extra cap. If you don't use a kickstand and forget about the hazards of leaning the bike against a cactus, these bags will puncture easily even if inside a pannier. Other bikers use rigid containers which can be folded when empty, and are sold under the brand name, "Reliance." These hold up quite well, but if you fold them

down very often when empty they eventually will spring a leak along the crease. The advantage of either of these is that they carry from one to two gallons of water. By using two of them in the front panniers for balance you can fill them according to need. If such large quantities of water are not needed, some people simply buy one quart or even one gallon containers of juice or spring water (for later usage as water containers) from local grocery stores and keep them in panniers in an upright position. The lids are then taped for extra insurance against leakage. These can be thrown away at the end of the tour.

4.   Tortilla Cooker. - This is a name I've given this very handy cooking utensil that takes up little room in the pannier. It's a flat 5" x 9" wire grid with a handle. It is perfect for warming up tortillas or making toast over the open fire or stove. I found mine in the kitchen department of a K-Mart type store and a friend found his in a Chinese grocery store in San Francisco. They are sold as cheese graters.

5.   Mesh Bags.- These come in various sizes and are great for carrying fresh tortillas, bread, or other squishables out on top of the pannier. Their use avoids using plastic bags that "sweat" and make dough of your bread. The bags usually close with drawstrings at the top. Mini-size bungees will secure the corners to your load. I find them in Pay 'n Save type stores sold as washing machine bags for women's nylons.

6.   Biodegradable Soap. - It only takes a cup or two of boiling water to do dishes. Personal hygiene around the camp can go a long way toward keeping one healthy.

7.   Wash'n Dry Towelettes. - With just a few drops of water to really get a cleansing effect, these can help minimize water used in washing-up efforts.

8.   Visor. - On hot days in Baja there can be a tremendous amount of radiated and reflected sunshine. A visor under the helmet, worn on the road and around camp, can help protect your face from sunburn.

Mountain Biking Tips

Much of what has been written about riding techniques for mountain bikers has little practicality for the touring cyclist. When these machines are loaded like beasts of burden they respond like same and travel becomes MIGHTY SLOW. There's no jumping ditches here. Just remember, however, it's still faster biking than hiking and with all that gear on your back, I can't imagine carrying along gallons of water as well! For the touring biker, the following tips may be helpful:

1.   Distribute the weight over the front and rear racks. There are suggested ratios to use but, when dealing with water at 8.3 pounds per gallon, much is dictated by where you can fit it all in. I generally put the water in the front two panniers (small ones so the containers are snug and don't flop around) and this weight varies with usage.   The handlebar bag is reserved for a camera and small odds and ends. Camping gear (tent, pad and sleeping bag) goes in one back pannier while cooking gear, one bag of clothes and food go in the other. A

toilet kit fits in one outside pocket and a quart fuel bottle in the other. Even though fuel is in a metal container, keep it separate, if possible, as it somehow always gives off a gas odor and/or taste to the other contents. If more food must be carried, then the sleeping bag goes up on top of the back rack. By all means, cinch the panniers tightly to the racks. This will prevent bouncing, which can eventually break the rack, and aids in stabilizing the bike. Even though the bike feels like a Mack truck at first, the load amazingly moves on down the road, giving a very stable and secure ride. Secure as many water bottles directly to the bike frame as possible.

2.   Lowering the seat for the downhills is good advice, but I have yet to see any touring cyclist do this, or even be able to, with gear stacked up on the back rack.

3.   A bad habit of mine is to run with my tires underinflated. When the road is good and hardpacked, it is a good idea to pump them up for more efficiency. In letting air out for rocky, sandy or washboard surfaces, care must be exerted. Letting out too much air allows the tire to bottom out on the rim. This can pinch the tube, causing a fine "fang" cut.

4.   Numb Hands. - This is not an unusual complaint from riders. One remedy is to loosen the hand brake bolts and slighty rotate the levers. Likewise, a slight rotation of the handlebars themselves will provide a new hand position and thus, relief for sore hands. Sometimes these adjustments need to be made once a day. Once a nerve is pinched, the hands can be numb for several days.

5.   There are specially made mountain biking shoes that serve well where walking-the-bike is often required. One set of biking shoes can serve the whole tour, while sandals or thongs may be used for evenings or beach days.

6.   Descents with a loaded bike can require good, slow riding skills. To keep the bike under control, the brakes, when used, must be skillfully used. Dodging rocks, holes and ruts takes a quick eye, concentration, anticipation and some very

heavy steering. Moving your bottom back and off the seat a little, while keeping the body low, helps maintain control. Unloaded bikes jump all over the road, but a loaded bike will go where you steer it. Therefore, control is essential if disaster is to be avoided.

7.   Because of the heavy load, the chain seldom gets up on that big chain wheel and the mid and lower gears see the most usage. When approaching a sandy stretch, gear down before hitting it. Keep your pedaling effort steady and maintain momentum. It it's a short stretch, you can muscle your way through, but if the traverse has any length at all, it's technique that will get you through. Unless you are on an incline, the lowest gear will probably be too low and you will have difficulty maintaining steady forward motion as can be done with a higher gear. Being steady and consistent in power expended is most important when going through sand.

8.   A riding technique you will automatically develop, without thinking, is that of constantly looking down the road ahead and evaluating what you see in terms of your course. You will soon find yourself looking even further ahead and making course decisions as this technique develops. The roads are often one lane with two tracks which four-wheeled vehicles have made, leaving a high center which is often of soft sand. By looking ahead, you can determine if a lane shift is needed and prepare to make a deliberate turn through the high center soft sand without the bike going out from under you. I find that such an upset can happen more often when using the lighter street tires.

9.   Because of the weight on board, the bike immediately looses momentum on the slightest uphill rise. After you've quickly shifted to your lowest gear, you may mentally have to reconcile yourself to the fact that it's OK to walk-the-bike. Some cyclists have a hard time with this.

10.   Shift the chain up to a bigger chain ring when cresting a hill to take up chain slack. A slack chain can fall or bounce in between the chain stay and tire (especially with the big

knobby tires). This can cause the wheel to lock and you and your bike will make a very sudden stop!

11.   When out in the boonies, miles and perhaps days away from assistance, if urgently needed, one becomes much more conservative in riding style and technique. I have heard people decry the use of a helmet because there is no traffic and the riding is so slow. To the contrary, a helmet is even more important in the boonies because you can still fall off a bike for any number of reasons. A head injury miles away from effective help may be too much for your companions to handle. How fast and the ease with which you reached your destination are of little importance when weighed against your well being and the fun you had in getting there safely.

12.   If you have a mountain bike and have felt the exhilaration of heading out across the open countryside with a mere water bottle and lunch in a fanny pack, it probably doesn't sound like much fun to ride a loaded touring bike. I no longer feel the excitement of a quick, responsive machine. Instead I get a feeling of incredulity over a good touring bike's durability and the resulting possibilities of places I might explore.

Mary Sinclair and Colin Warner, dirt road near Catavina

BIKE REPAIRS

On our Baja 1000 journey, Mari and I didn't even take along a tool kit as such. We had tire changing equipment and the Allen wrench to loosen the handle bars. We had an extra tube, but not an extra tire. Many think this absurd, saying it's like going to the desert with only one small water bottle. I am not very concerned about breakdowns. They have been rare in past experience and it's inevitable that if you carry eight pounds of tools and parts, something will break that you didn't bring. Murphy's Law says so. You can't carry a whole bike shop. I'd rather carry water. I am prepared mentally to just wait and deal with the problem when it occurs.

On a group tour where equipment is spread out equally among everyone, I do indeed carry some essential tools and parts. With many bikes in the party, the possibility of some kind of trouble greatly increases. I will say, though, that our "breakdowns" have been minor and some very creative bike repairs were executed so that riders could continue the trip. I can't help but repeat myself: mountain bikes are incredibly durable.

By far the most common failure has simply been flat tires. By and large the wind keeps the road bed free of thorns. Off the road it is another matter. This is why I suggest carrying the bike (minus bags) off the road to the campsite. I was able to enjoy the entire Baja 1000 trip without a flat.

Another problem concerning tires is that of sidewall cuts. Several areas of Baja have very sharp, shifting volcanic rocks which continually cut into tires. Knobbies will take care of most of this, but sidewalls can acquire some long cuts. Take along some booting to keep from damaging tubes. Booting is any protective material inserted between tire and tube to block the tube from bulging out the cut in the tire.

The next most common failure is rack failure. Occasionally a rack will break, but much more often they simply come apart due to loosened bolts--even after Locktite was applied! Once underway, one needs to make it a routine to check all nuts/bolts on the bike daily or every other day. They simply work loose. Racks collapse, water bottle cages fall off, and even bolts on the chain rings have fallen out. Preventive maintenance helps a bike endure the long journey ahead.

Most books on equipment have long lists of tools to carry and you have probably already discovered what to you is useful and what is not. The following are additional items that I've found helpful for either paved or dirt road touring.

1.   Hose Clamps. - Include several sizes of hose clamps but lean to the smaller ones which will fit racks. Many a trip has been saved because these handy items were able to hold a broken rack together.

2.   Locktite. - Apply Locktite to nuts and bolts before getting underway. Also apply it to any nuts or bolts replaced during the trip.

3.   Extra Nuts/Bolts. - Check the bolt sizes used on your bike. Take some matching sets in the various sizes used.

4.   Moleskin. - Moleskin works well and is easy to install as a booting material against sidewall cuts.

5.   Tweezers. - Tweezers are almost a necessity in desert areas. Many multi-purpose pocket knives, such as Swiss Army knives, are equipped with tweezers, among other tools, and such a knife is a good investment. Use the tweezers to pull thorns from tires, being careful not to break off the thorn in the tire. Tweezers are also handy for extracting thorns from people.

6.   Extra Pannier Hooks. - There are several different pannier attachment systems involving hooks. Carry along some extra hooks which match your system for replacement, or for additional top and bottom attachments.

7.   Bailing Wire. - Bailing wire is the universal panacea for most repairs. Especially recommended by shade-tree

mechanics, it has many uses around a touring bicycle. One example is the shoring-up of broken, or heavily overloaded racks.

8.   <u>Duct Tape.</u> - Duct tape can be used as a booting material inside a tire casing. It also may be used for other patching needs.

9.   <u>12" Crescent Wrench</u>. - If you really must remove that freewheel, or tighten a headset, this wrench will do it. Also note: there is little in the desert to which a pocket vise may be attached.

10.   <u>Other Spare Parts.</u> - I usually include as spares, two or three tire tubes, a spare tire, a freewheel, cables, rear derailleur and chain.

....well, that's life.....

Bike Shops

Many bikers are surprised to learn that there are bicycle shops in Baja. Although the distances can be very long between these shops, amazing things are done by Mexicans for an ailing machine. There are several quality shops in both Tijuana and Ensenada.

At 187 miles south of the border is San Quintin, with at least two shops. These may not have the exotic touring accessories, but do have the basics. After that, it is a long way to Loreto before another shop appears. Even the Loreto shop can be questionable as the business seems to be functioning on one trip and not the next. A sure bet is the well-stocked shop in Ciudad Constitucion. La Paz has several shops and Cabo San Lucas has one.

Out of all the groups I have taken to Baja, no one has ever had to quit the trip because of an unrepairable bicycle. There have been very few serious breakdowns. The most common problem is, simply, flat tires. I always recommend heavy duty tires and tubes. They give a smoother ride on rough roads and they also hold up well against the pesky thorn situation. With regard to thorns, even the kevlar tire liners are not 100% effective.

Public Telephones and Transportation

Telephoning into Mexico

Only A.T.&T. lines reach Mexico. You cannot call using M.C.I. or Sprint. If you don't have A.T.&T. service, you can get an A.T.&T. line by dialing 10ATT then 1 and then the number. Telephone numbers in Mexico are subject to change. When an office is moved, the telephone (number) stays with the old office, and the new office then has a new telephone number. Remember, if dialing from the U. S., dial 70 then the area code and number for Northern Baja. Dial 01152, area code and number for Baja Sur.

Bus Service in Baja

There are several bus lines providing service between Tijuana and Cabo San Lucas (with a transfer in La Paz). A one way ticket to La Paz is approximately $25 and takes 26 hours with two drivers spelling each other. The price for the bicycle is negotiable. The Central Bus Station of Tijuana is located southeast of Tijuana Airport, telephone (706) 686-9060. Tres Estrellas de Oro (3 Stars of Gold) and Transportes Aguila (Eagle Transports) is (706) 686-9515, ext. 112. Autotransportes de Baja California (ABC) is (706) 686-9060.

Bicycles are taken as luggage on a space available basis, so it is wise to go a little early, purchase your ticket and indicate you have a bike. You make your seat selection at the time of ticket purchase and seats toward the front are recommended, as the toilets at the back of the bus begin to smell by journey's end.

If more than two bikes are to be loaded, or if you're traveling at holiday time and it is crowded, you should be prepared to disassemble your bike into as small a package as possible. One way to do this is to take along two giant size garbage bags and tape. Take off the bike wheels, placing one on each side of the frame, turn the handlebars, lower the seat, take off the pedals and try not to lose them. Place these items in the garbage bags end to end and tape the bags shut. Most of the time you can take this package to the bus loading zone yourself and place it in the luggage compartment. Once the bus is loaded, the luggage compartment is left undisturbed and the bikes will ride well if they are packaged well to begin with. If you aren't planning to ride your bike to the station, you can do all this packaging before hand and save a lot of time. If you arrive in San Diego and use the Mexicoach service to Tijuana, your bike will already be boxed and ready to go.

Besides being very inexpensive, the bus is safe. I've taken the bus on many occasions and feel the drivers are just as professional and competent as U.S. drivers. It was after several trips that I finally discovered where the second driver appears from or disappears to. The big buses have luggage compartments, one on each side of the bus. However, only the right side is used for luggage. The compartment on the driver's side houses the off-duty driver. It is decked out with a mattress, blanket, pillow, and a two-way intercom to the driver. When one driver gets tired, they switch. There has to be a radio down there to drown out the road noise. The bus is always an adventure in some way for it's hard to go for 26 hours in Baja without something entertaining happening.

If returning from La Paz on the bus, the bags and tape routine work fine, as boxes are nearly non-existent.

Airline Service

Airline schedules and fares to Baja change frequently, so you should call the airline directly or check with your travel agent. In recent years some very good fares have been offered. These are on a joint fare, or extended fare, basis between a U.S. carrier serving Los Angeles or San Francisco from out of state, with a transfer to Aero Mexico to Baja. Currently bicycles have been charged $25 from Los Angeles and San Francisco, but are taken at no extra charge from Tijuana. Service is provided by the following airlines.

Aero California (800) 522-1516
Daily flights from Tijuana to La Paz

PSA (800) 854-2902
Various flights from San Francisco to San Jose del Cabo on a non-daily basis.
Various flights from Los Angeles to San Jose del Cabo on a non-daily basis

Mexicana (800) 531-7921
Daily flights from Los Angeles to San Jose Del Cabo.
Daily flights from Tijuana to La Paz.
Various flights from San Francisco to San Jose del Cabo on a non-daily basis.

Aero Mexico (800) 237-6639
Daily flights from Los Angeles to La Paz.
Various flights from Los Angeles to San Jose del Cabo and
Loreto on a non-daily basis.
Various flights from Tijuana to Loreto, La Paz and San Jose
del Cabo on a non-daily basis.

Ferry Service

After completing a Baja journey, cyclists often wish to extend
their Mexican sojourn through mainland Mexico. Using the
ferry is an inexpensive means toward accomplishing this.

Ferry service between the peninsula and mainland Mexico is
often late or off-schedule once underway. Go prepared with
some extra food. The ferry food can be expensive and
monotonous. Go to the ferry ticket office and purchase your
ticket for the departure date you want. Bicycles will be loaded
in the automobile section, which is locked once underway.
Therefore, you should carry with you whatever you may need
during the passage. Have your gear organized before taking
the bikes down for loading, as the air on the automobile deck
is quite foul with exhaust and diesel fumes.

Passengers can select salon, a reclining chair, or tourist class
(which offers bunk beds on a lower deck). Some ferries also
offer cabins (cabin with bed and bathroom) or *especial* (deluxe
cabins on the upper deck). For cabins, go a day before to
reserve.

The following schedule will give you an idea of frequency and
length of time for the crossing. Always check ahead for
changes.

Santa Rosalia - Guaymas (Tuesday, Thursday, Sunday)
Leaves Santa Rosalia 11 p.m. arriving 7 a.m.
Leaves Guaymas 10 a.m. arriving 6:30 p.m.
Ferry ticket office is in the terminal building.

La Paz - Topolobampo
Leaves La Paz 8 p.m. Thursday and Sunday, arriving 4 a.m.

Leaves Topolobampo 10 a.m. Tuesday and Friday, arriving 6 p.m.
La Paz ferry ticket office is at Avenida Francisco Madero at Victoria.

La Paz - Mazatlan (daily)
Leaves at 5 p.m., arriving 9 a.m. the following morning.

La Paz - Puerto Vallarta (Tuesday)
Leaves at noon, arriving the following noon.

Cabo San Lucas - Puerto Vallarta
Leaves Cabo Sunday and Wednesday at 4 p.m., arriving at 10 a.m.
Leaves Puerto Vallarta Saturday and Tuesday at 4 p.m., arriving at 10 a.m.
Ferry ticket office is in the terminal building.

Getting There

Whether you plan to start bicycling from Tijuana, take a flight from the Tijuana airport, or get to the Tijuana bus station, you need to get to the border. There are several options available. You can bicycle the 21 miles from downtown San Diego, take a bus and bicycle 5 miles to the border, or use one of several public transportation options.

By Bicycle - San Diego to Tijuana

These directions cover bicycle routes to the border from the San Diego airport, AMTRAK terminal and/or bus stations. All of these terminals are in close proximity, hence the similarities in directions.

Lindbergh Field International Airport

When leaving the airport, follow signs saying "Downtown" which will lead you onto the bike path along Harbor Drive going south.

AMTRAK Terminal

When leaving the terminal by the south exit and into the parking lot, go right on Broadway (west) to the water's edge - this is Harbor Drive. Turn left on Harbor Drive and go south.

Greyhound Bus Station

Again, head for Broadway turning right (west) until you intersect Harbor Drive. Turn left to go south.

The following road log describes the trip. Distances shown are in miles.

0.0   Lindbergh Field International Airport

0.3 Harbor Dr. going south - bike path available.

2.8 Junction with Broadway, where travelers by AMTRAK or bus come in. Continue straight on Harbor Drive.

3.1 Harbor Dr. automatically swings left - now Market Street.

3.2 Right - on Pacific Highway.

3.3 Left - back onto Harbor Dr. Follow Harbor Dr. to Civic Center Drive in National City.

8.1 Right - on Civic Center.

8.2 Left - immediately on Cleveland.

8.9 Left - on 24th St. Pass under I-5.

9.4 Right - on National City Blvd.

10.4 National City Blvd. becomes Broadway.

11.0 Right onto "E" St. You' re now in Chula Vista. Cross over I-5.

11.5 Left onto Bay Blvd., which makes a few jogs, but stays west of I-5 and becomes Anita St.

14.8 Right - on Frontage Road.

15.1 Follow the Bay Route Bikeway (signed) to 19th St.

15.9 Left - on Palm Ave. - this crosses I-5. Fast moving traffic will be turning right onto the freeway entrance.

17.2 Right onto Beyer Blvd.

18.5 Crosses under Freeway 117.

20.0   Crosses over Freeway 805.

20.1   Right - E. Beyer Blvd., which goes downhill and curves left at the bottom. A left turn at the East Beyer intersection picks up the Otay Mesa route (see Alternate Bike Route).

21.2   Straight - at junction with San Ysidro Blvd. This is the main shopping street for last minute U.S. goods needed or money exchange. Going straight at this intersection puts you on a bridge over the freeway. Sign will say "International Border."

21.3   Left - after the bridge. Sign says "Camiones." This will put you on a pedestrian walkway over the border. Walk or ride, depending on how many people there are.

To continue bicycling, see **Getting Through Tijuana, Tijuana to Ensenada, Tour No. 1**

Getting to the Tijuana Airport/Bus Station

Once over the border, within the next block is a big lot on the right full of taxis. This may well be your first "cultural" encounter - negotiating a taxi ride up to the airport or to the bus station. Most of the taxis are big, American-made cars and there are some station wagons. Be sure to settle on a price before you pack the bike and get in.

Should you insist on bicycling to the airport, follow the well-marked signs "Aeropuerto" but, be forewarned, there is a "wall" of a hill to get up. The road to the bus station goes below the hill.

If coming from the airport, the road is well marked with signs for San Diego and you get to go down the wall. When approaching all the border traffic lines, stay right, pass all the cars and go to the front where the stop lights are. Take the first exit right.

Otay Mesa Border Crossing - Alternate Bike Route

The preferred route to the Tijuana Airport, bus station, and possibly even the *libre* road to Ensenada, is through the recently opened Otay Mesa border crossing. This station is open 6 a.m. to 10 p.m. Many trucks use this route to avoid the busy and congested San Yisdro route, but the road is wide with a good shoulder. This route also has a hill to contend with, but it is much more negotiable on a bike, not nearly as steep, and certainly there is less traffic and fewer turns to make.

The following road log describes the trip. Refer back to the previous road log, picking up the San Ysidro directions at mile 20.1. Distances shown are in miles.

20.1   Junction of Beyer Blvd. and E. Beyer Blvd. Left - on Otay Mesa Rd. (E. Beyer Blvd. goes right).

22.0   Right - at top of the hill at Tee junction, still called Otay Mesa Rd., or Highway 117. This road can be busy, but has shoulder most of the way. There are parallel side roads to the right, but some portions are not paved.

29.8   Border. After crossing, stay to the far right and take the truck route if heading to the airport. This is a little shorter than following the airport signs. For the bus station, continue straight. Watch for signs to Ensenada.

31.0   Right onto a main road.   Sign for airport and Ensenada.

31.4   Parque de La Amistad on right.

31.6   Traffic circle - a hard right to airport.

31.7   On around the circle, exiting on signed road for Mexicali. Begin downhill - this is a one-way road.

33.4   Bus station on left.

Continue straight for Ensenada - the road is well marked with signs. There are a couple of substantial hills to climb. This route, however, completely avoids the downtown congestion of Tijuana unless you are going through early in the morning.

By Bus and Bicycle - San Diego to Tijuana

San Diego Transit

This option takes advantage of a city bus equipped with a bike rack that goes within 4 miles of the San Ysidro border.

Find the bus stop on Broadway directly across the street from the AMTRAK station. There are different lines with bike racks but wait for #901, (not #9) which only goes as far as the

Coronado Bridge). This bus comes by approximately every half hour. Have bike bags off and be ready to load the bike on the back of the bus. The wheels fit into rail type slots. The locking mechanism is attached to the lower tube where there is usually a pump or water bottle holder attached. Therefore, be prepared with the correct tool if any of these need to be removed. The rack I used was very greasy and the attachment part was not padded. So if trying to save a paint job on your frame, have along an old rag to pad with. Bus fare is $1.00 in change. Bills are not accepted. Take #901 to the end of the line, which is Palm Ave. at Hollister. The ride takes about 1 hour and 10 minutes.

The following road log describes the trip. Distances shown are in miles.

0.0   From end of bus line, continue straight on Palm Ave.

0.5   Right on Beyer Blvd.

0.8   Crosses under Freeway 117.

3.3   Crosses over Freeway 805.

3.4   Junction with E. Beyer Blvd. Turn to the right for the San Ysidro crossing, or take Otay Mesa Rd. to the left for the Otay Mesa crossing.   Follow directions given under BY BICYCLE - SAN DIEGO TO TIJUANA.

San Diego Trolley

The San Diego trolley is a unique service running between downtown San Diego and the San Ysidro border crossing. It has several stops along the line, so besides taking tourists back and forth to the border, it also functions as a commuter service. It is especially convenient if you are arriving in San Diego by air, bus or train. Because the service is relatively new and run on an honor-self-service system, there are currently some restrictions on taking bicycles aboard which make it very inconvenient for out-of-town cyclists.

To put your bike on the trolley legally, you need a pass. It costs $3.00 and must be purchased from the AYH (American Youth Hostel) in person. Since there are no ticket takers at the trolley, you need to go to the AYH office at 1031 India St. and bring a snapshot of yourself. India St. is only a block from the trolley station and five blocks from the Greyhound bus depot. The office hours are 9 a.m. to 4:30 p.m. The phone number is (619) 239-2644. For current regulations you may want to call the trolley at (619) 231-8549. Usage of the trolley excludes bikes on weekdays between 6 - 9 a.m. and 3 - 5 p.m., 11 a.m. - 5 p.m. on Saturdays, but the trolley is open all day to bikes on Sundays. Tickets are currently $1.50. Perhaps with time the pass will be available for advance purchase by mail.

San Diego County Transit System

Some county buses with bike racks that go to and from Tecate are available. Ask for a Southeast Rural Bus Schedule from: County of San Diego, Dept. of Public Works, Transportation Operations Section, Bldg. 2, 5555 Overland Ave., San Diego 92123. Current fare is $2.00 from the Parkway Plaza. For further information call (619) 478-5875, or outside San Diego, call the operator and ask for the toll free number, ZE 7-5875, open 7-11 a.m. and 1- 5 p.m. weekdays. The bus doesn't run on weekends or holidays.

Commercial Bus Service - San Diego to Tijuana

Mexicoach

Another option, and perhaps the least amount of hassle, is to use the service provided by Mexicoach. Employing full-sized buses, you can board at the AMTRAK station for a ride over the border, where you'll be transferred to a taxi (included in the price) to the airport. They accept bicycles at no extra charge, preferably boxed, though a tip to the cab driver might be expected. There is daily scheduled service between San

Diego and Tijuana and one-way tickets are $15.00. Call (619) 232-5049 for schedule and information.

Tijuana Transportation Service

Still another alternative that accepts bicycles is the Tijuana Transportation Service running between downtown San Diego and directly to the Tijuana Airport. You can pick it up at the Hotel San Diego, 339 West Broadway. One-way fare is $10.00 and a round trip discount is given. You need to make reservations 24 hours in advance by calling (619) 428-6624, or in California, (800) 854-3913.

3

THE TOURS

General

As was described in   Chapter 1, this chapter contains descriptions of 16 tours as follows:

A.   Five short tours just across the U. S. Border. See "Day Rides Near the Border" (Tour Numbers 1 - 5). These tours may be combined to form longer rides if desired.

B.   Seven tours which may be taken individually, in combinations, or as one long chain down the full length of the Baja peninsula from Tijuana to Cabo San Lucas. Public transportation to the point(s) of entry of each tour, or tour combination, is described. See "Transpeninsular Tours" (Tour Numbers 6 - 12).

C.   Four mountain bike, or back country tours for those who enjoy a challenge as well as the rugged country environment. See "Rough Stuff (Off-Highway) Tours" (Tour Numbers 13 - 16).

I have standardized the format used with each tour as follows:

1.   Tour Number; Tour Title. The tours are numbered in consecutive order. The tours are titled in terms of the point of departure and the destination point. While the titles and sequence of tours run from north to south, the routes may be traversed, of course, in either direction.

2. Length. This item consists of the total length of the tour in kilometers and miles.

3. Time Required: The time required to complete each tour is estimated for typical, self-contained, touring cyclists, who are comfortable at 40 to 50 miles per day. You may adjust this estimate up or down to suit your own comfort zone. All estimates assume bicycle travel is in one direction only.

4. Season: This item states the months of the year which I recommend as optimum for the particular tour.

5. Difficulty: This item categorizes routes into three categories: average, difficult and rugged; in addition, a short description of route characteristics is included. The ratings are based upon the terrain of the routes and not on logistics, i.e., ease of access, availability of services, etc. For the mountain bike routes, a trip may receive a more severe rating because of just one small section of the route which is rugged.

6. General: This item provides a general description of the countryside to be traversed, and general characteristics thereof which might be of interest to the touring cyclist.

7. Point of Entry: This item provides a description of the northern point of entry for each tour. Population, major sources of income, climate, services, points of scenic and/or historical interest are described.

8. Logistics: This item provides information concerning public transportation available to the tour points of departure/destination, any special equipment, food, etc. which should be used or carried, and the general availability of services and accommodations along the route.

9. Map: A brief map (not intended for navigational usage) accompanies each tour. In addition, where large population centers must be traversed, a street route map through the city or town is included.

10. Route Log: The Route Log commences at the northern point of departure for each tour. Key landmarks or mileage points are defined from that point and include, in the order shown:

a). Distance of the landmark from the tour point of departure in either kilometers or miles, as applicable (this is determined by mileage post call-outs along the route).

b). Cumulative mileage shown as: xxxS/xxxN. This notation refers to the mileage accumulated from the tour point of departure and proceeding south (S), and the mileage accumulated from the destination point and proceeding north (N).

c). Elevation in feet above sea level.

d). Pertinent information concerning the designated landmark or mileage point. Oftentimes this information may consist of the notation "Road Left," or Road Right." This notation indicates a side road to the left or right of the main route where off-highway camping might be desirable. Using a side road avoids going over fences when there are some, and helps stay clear of the thorns. Unless noted, all "Roads Left" or "Roads Right" are dirt and don't have gates. Remember to carry your bike from the side road to your campsite as a further precaution against tires beset with thorns.

The elevations shown in the Route Log were measured with my fairly simple altimeter, which was uncompensated for the ambient barometric pressure. These elevations are just for fun and reference. This log should dispel any illusions that the peninsula is flat!

Kilometer posts appear beside the road from Ensenada south. However, they are not continuous in numbering all the way to the Cape, but go in sections. For example, Ensenada to San Quintin is 198 KM, then the post numbering starts over again. In the State of Baja California the numbers get larger going south. In the State of Baja California Sur they get smaller going south.

In case you have forgotten, a kilometer (KM) measures 0.62 miles. When identifying a landmark, i.e., town, hill, road or service in the Route Log, the kilometer post just prior to that point is noted. Thus the landmark may be a short way past the particular KM post noted.

Day Rides Near the Border

This section consists of five tours, all adjacent to the Southern California (U.S.) - Baja California border, which may be traversed in one or two days. These tours can be combined to form loop trips, or longer one-way trips augmented by public transportation. The tours included are listed below:

Tour No. 1 - Tijuana to Ensenada

Tour No. 2 - Tecate to Mexicali

Tour No. 3 - Mexicali to San Felipe

Tour No. 4 - San Felipe to Ensenada

Tour No. 5 - Ensenada to Tecate

The Northern Baja Loop

Tours 1 through 5 are often combined in sequence to form the Northern Baja Loop. The loop is about 500 miles in length. It can be traversed in ten days to two weeks with much simpler logistics than some of the transpeninsular tours. In fact, if you have less than a week, or if time runs out, bus service from any of the tour terminals to your starting point is very good.

For me, the biggest draw of the Northern Baja Loop is that it can be done at a time of year when most of the Transpeninsular Highway is too hot. Spring and fall have pleasant temperatures with blooming plants and flowers, especially in spring. Fall can play tricks with the weather on the Sea of Cortez side, but usually calms down after September.

The loop offers a good taste of Baja with a mix of lush and prosperous agricultural valleys, high chaparral, plains with mountain vistas, unlikely basins of water, dry, desolate desert areas and views both of the Sea of Cortez and Pacific Ocean. Interspersed with the varied and challenging terrain are the major cities of Baja, with the exception of La Paz (which is farther south). Some remain typically Mexican in character while others are resigned to the task of catering to the whims of tourists.

The tour from Tijuana to Tecate is not described and is not recommended because of very heavy traffic conditions. The first 11 miles east of Tijuana are wonderful, on a wide-laned divided roadway. However, the three lanes drop to two at 9.2 miles and from two down to one each way at mile 11.9. From there the narrow roadway, crowded with trucks, buses and other vehicles, steadily climbs to Tecate.

Casey Patterson on a fast, downhill run

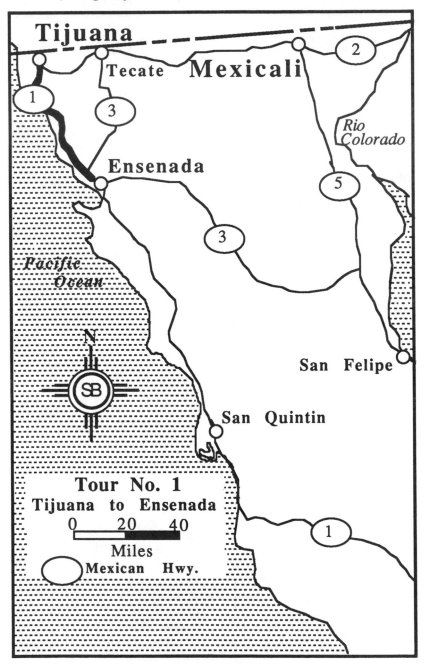

Tijuana

Tecate Mexicali

Rio
Colorado

Ensenada

Pacific
Ocean

San Felipe

San Quintin

Tour No. 1
Tijuana to Ensenada
0   20   40
Miles
Mexican Hwy.

TOUR NO. 1 TIJUANA TO ENSENADA

Length: 115 KM / 70 Miles

Time Required: 1 or 2 days

Season: September to May

Difficulty: Average

Traffic does build up in late afternoon. Leaving Tijuana, or "TJ," one is faced with nearly a four mile climb followed by a long, sloping downhill to the coast. There the old road parallels the *cuota* (toll) road and scenic coastline for nearly 24 miles. At La Mision the route turns inland with nearly 10 miles of more up than down. Back to the coast again, it is an easy ride into Ensenada.

General:

Part of the attraction of this ride is its scenic beauty, variety of terrain and low traffic, considering that the route is connecting two major Baja cities.

Point of Entry: Tijuana.

With a population of over a million, Tijuana is the fourth largest city in Mexico and is still growing. Those knowing of its colorful history probably do not have a correct current impression because in recent years the city has undergone a major face lift. There has been some shift of its economic dependency on tourist dollars to manufacturing and commerce. Tourism, of course, is still important and strides in quality and diversification have been made. As a result, souvenirs and merchandise to suit nearly all tastes are readily available.

It's cleaner than it used to be. Modern housing has popped up throughout the city to replace many of the cardboard shanties. Tijuana, for all its progress, is still a big city of a foreign country and that contrast hits you with the first wheel over the border.

Logistics:

An early crossing makes it easy to negotiate the streets and find the *libre* road to Ensenada before the traffic builds up. There are several motels on the U.S. side in San Ysidro for the pre-tour overnight. A hostel is located at Imperial Beach, 5 miles from the border, for an inexpensive overnight (619) 423-8039. There is also a fine new hostel located in Tijuana should you want to sightsee and enjoy the city. When on a bicycle, seeing Tijuana just as it awakens is a good time to ride through. See "GETTING THERE" for information concerning bike routes and public transportation on the San Diego side of the border.

Getting Through Tijuana - Border Crossing, San Ysidro Route

Approaching Tijuana via the San Ysidro border crossing, you will most likely be happily waved through the crossing by a friendly Mexican official, who, at most, may ask how far you plan to go, just out of curiosity. Use the far right lane.

A quick look at a Tijuana city map and you'll probably suspect there is a more direct way of getting onto the *libre* (free) road to Ensenada. There are two similar routes given here (Options 1 and 2) which I think are fairly easy to follow. Finding a sign when you want one, or expecting one, is always a problem in Mexico, and spending time chasing your tail in Tijuana isn't the most pleasant way to start the trip.

While looking at that Tijuana map you'll probably also notice Mexico 1-D - a fine looking road, much more along the coast than Mexico 1. Don't be tempted. This a divided freeway and toll road prohibited to bicyclists. There is a day, however, when this road is made available to cyclists (see "Major Annual Rides" in the Appendix).

This section of the road log is given in miles since the kilometer posts are few and far between and don't show up at all in the city. They will be noted when they do appear.

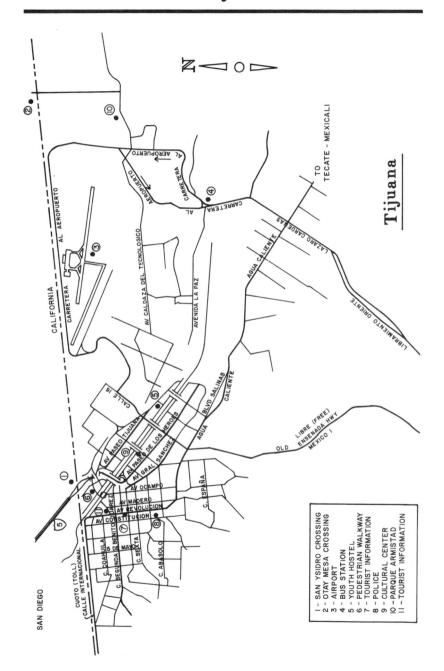

Getting Through Tijuana - Option 1

This route is suggested if you are crossing the border and traversing Tijuana after traffic has built up. After crossing the border, stay to the right. Just before the big taxi lot is the pedestrian walkway, a big wide thoroughfare. You'll cross a divided street with the pedestrian overpass right in front of you. Beside the steps is a ramp for wheeling up the bike. The overpass crosses the usually non-flowing Rio Tijuana. The overpass also crosses over the highway leading from the border and passes Ave. Revolucion in a few blocks.

Descend the pedestrian walkway. As you exit, rows of tourist *tiendas* will be in front of you. Stay to the far left of these and walk your bike one block beside the highway you just crossed over. That highway will be on your left and the little shops on your right.

Turn Left - at the first road. This is Ave. Ocampo, though there is no sign until the next block with the stop light. This first block is dirt with *tiendas* on either side. Stay on Ocampo some 11 blocks.

Turn Left - on Blvd. Agua Caliente. This intersection has a stoplight. Casa de Nutricion is on the left corner and a *pinturas* store is across the street with a big billboard sign of paint cans. Going straight, the smaller road becomes Ave. Agua Caliente and goes uphill.

Turn Right - at Kentucky Fried Chicken - if you get to the bullring you've gone too far.

Getting Through Tijuana - Option 2

0.0 Miles - Cross San Ysidro border before 8 a.m. and you'll have very little traffic. Follow big green signs saying Ensenada - Cuota. This makes a big circle with traffic exiting and entering. Use caution. First, stay to the right, then swing to an inner left lane. It's well signed, but travel's difficult when traffic's heavy. Left on Ave.Revolucion - the second left turn at the time of recording this log. There are 4 white signs saying "El Centro". This is the main road through the heart of the downtown shopping district.

Left - automatically the road swings left at a big Coca Cola sign and is now called Agua Caliente.

3.5 Miles - Turn right at Kentucky Fried Chicken - this is Ave. 16 de Septiembre, but there is no sign to tell you this. Road begins to climb soon after the turn. There will also be a sign for Ave. 16 de Septiembre.

Route Log - Tijuana to Ensenada

3.5 Miles (3.5S / 68.7N; el.120 ft.)
Turn right at Kentucky Fried Chicken - this is Ave. 16 de Septiembre, but there is no sign to tell you this. Road begins to climb soon after the turn and you'll find a street sign for Septiembre within the first block.

6.8 Miles (6.8S / 65.4N)
Sign for Ensenada, "100 KM."

6.9 Miles (6.9S / 65.3 N)
Left at Y - for Rosarito/Ensenada.

7.4 Miles (7.4S / 64.8N)
Top of hill followed by long downhill.

8.9 Miles (8.9S / 63.3 N)
Abarrotes and *loncheria.*

11.0 Miles; 16KM (11.0 S / 61.2 N)
First kilometer post we've noticed - 16 KM.

12.7 Miles (12.7S / 59.5N)
Abarrotes.

14.1 Miles; 20 KM 14.1S / 58.1N)
Several stores, *loncheria* and *panaderia.*

14.8 Miles; 21 KM (14.8S / 57.4N)
Sign for Popotla, 11 KM.

15.3 Miles; 22 KM (15.3S/ 56.9N)
Road crosses over toll road. Follow sign for Rosarito, a developed commercial area along the coast.

17.0 Miles; 24.7 KM (17.0S /55.2 N; el.100 ft.)
Rosarito - a developing community of services oriented to tourists. Rosarito spreads along the highway for several kilometers. Starting point for the Rosarito-Ensenada Ride (see "Major Annual Rides," Appendix).

17.4 Miles; 25.3 KM (17.4S / 54.8N)
La Playa Trailer Park - right.

17.6 Miles; 25.6 KM (17.6S / 54.6N)
Panaderia on right - bigger.

18.2 Miles; 26.6 KM (18.2S / 54.0N)
Panaderia on left.

18.4 Miles; 28 KM (18.4S / 53.8N)
More strip development.

19.4 Miles; 29.6 KM (19.4S / 52.8N)
Corona del Mar Trailer Park.

20.7 Miles; 31.7 KM (20.7S / 51.5N)
La Barca RV Park

21.0 Miles; 32.2 KM (21.0S / 51.2N)
Panaderia on right - leaving town.

22.7 Miles; 34.9 KM (22.7S / 49.5N)
Popotla - restaurant and bar which caters to tourists.

23.5 Miles; 36.2 KM (23.5S / 48.7)N)
Calafia - open camping on right until condos are built. Nice view of the coastline.

24.6 Miles; 38 KM (sign) (24.6S / 47.6N)
Santa Maria Trailer Park.

29.3 Miles; 45.5 KM (29.3S / 42.9N)
El Pescadero - *abarrotes, loncheria.*

30.8 Miles; 48.0 KM (30.8S / 41.4N)
Cantamar - *abarrotes, loncheria.*

31.6 Miles; 49.3 KM (31.6S / 40.6N)
Panaderia.

31.9 Miles; 49.7 KM (31.9S / 40.3N)
Sand dunes.

34.5 Miles; 53.9 KM (34.5S / 37.7N)
Open camping on right - no facilities.

35.1 Miles; 54.9 KM (35.1S / 37.1N)
Halfway House - restaurant overlooking the coastline.

35.6 Miles; 55.7 KM (35.6S / 36.6N)
Open camping on right for about 1 mile - on beach.   No facilities.

37.0 Miles; 58.0 KM (37.0S / 35.2N)
La Mision.

39.6 Miles; 62.2 KM (39.6S / 32.6N)
La Fonda Motel.

40.1 Miles; 63.0 KM (40.1S / 32.1N)
63 KM Post.

40.9 Miles; 64.3 KM (40.9S / 31.3N)
Road goes under the toll road, makes a short climb, leaves the coast.

42.6 Miles; 67.0 KM (42.6S / 29.6N)
Ejido la Mision.   Very small cluster of houses, *loncheria.*

Washouts have been a continuous problem, but more substantial bridges are now being built.

43.6 Miles; 68.6 KM (43.6S / 28.6N)
Small *abarrotes* - start climb.

46.0 Miles; 72.5 KM (46.0S / 26.2 N)
Top of hill.

50.8 Miles; 80.2 KM (50.8S / 21.4N)
Pop stop - beautiful area, but all fenced.   Camp with permission only.

51.0 Miles; 80.5 KM (51.0S / 21.2N)
Start climb.

53.0 Miles; 83.8 KM (53.0S / 19.2N)
Top of hill.

53.7 Miles; 84.9 KM (53.7S / 18.5N)
Road left.

54.3 Miles; 85.9 KM (54.3S / 17.9N)
Top of hill - long downhill ahead.

55.3 Miles; 87.5 KM (55.3S / 16.9N)
Road left to Valle de Guadalupe. 0.2 miles in on left there is a side road with camping possibilities - the rest is all fenced. El Junco, El Tigre, El Carmen - no services.

62.4 Miles; 98.9 KM (62.4S / 9.8N)
Old road goes to right - camping possibilities before reaching highway.

63.0 Miles; 99.9 KM (63.0S / 9.2N)
Junction with the toll road.

64.1 Miles; 101.7 KM (64.1S / 8.1N)
El Sausal - sprawling community with sizeable fish cannery.

65.1 Miles; 103.3 KM (65.1S / 7.1N)
Strip development - several markets and cafes.

66.2 Miles; 105.1 KM (66.2S / 6.0N)
Motel California and RV park.

68.4 Miles; 108.6 KM (68.4S / 3.8N)
Right - at sign for El Centro - entering Ensenada.

70.8 Miles; 112.5 KM (70.8S / 1.4N)
Right at Y - sign for Highway 1 and San Quintin says, "Go Left." However, it is a much more complicated route. Your road is now called Blvd. Lazaro Cardenas.

71.2 Miles; 113.1 KM (71.2S / 1.0N, El.10 ft.)
Plaza with three large head statues of past heros: Juarez, Carranza and Hidalgo. There are public rest rooms on either side of this nicely kept plaza.

71.6 Miles; 113.8 KM (71.6S / 0.6N)
Left turn for the La Pinta Hotel on Ave. Riviera and several other hotels, or to downtown Ensenada. The big white and gold trimmed building on the left was once a famous resort well known for its striking Mediterranean architecture. Called the Riviera del Pacifico, it is now used for public events.

72.2 Miles; 114.7 KM (72.2S / 0.0N)
Road swings left and is now called Calle Gral. Agustin San Gines (no sign). RV park with camping is on left, Motel La Fiesta is next door. A hospital is on the right after another block.

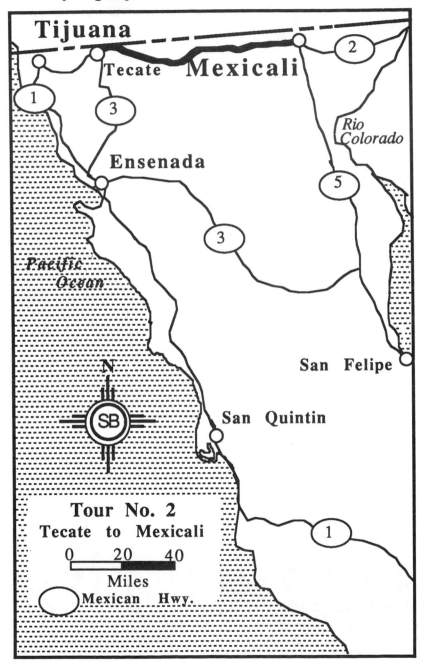

Tijuana

Tecate   Mexicali

Rio Colorado

Ensenada

Pacific Ocean

San Felipe

San Quintin

N

SB

Tour No. 2
Tecate   to   Mexicali

0   20   40

Miles

Mexican   Hwy.

TOUR NO. 2 - TECATE TO MEXICALI

Length: 130 KM / 80.6 Miles

Time Required: One to two days

Season: September to May. Can be cold
                      December, January, February

Difficulty: Average with lots of downhill
Shortly after leaving town the road gradually and steadily
climbs from the bowl shaped valley onto high open plains. If
it's windy, there is little protection along here. With a string of
small towns and other facilities, food is never too far away.
The highest point of this tour is reached near the town of La
Rumorosa, followed by the steepest and longest downhill of
Baja.   At the bottom, the landscape is nearly devoid of
vegetation yet supports a rather large shallow lake, through the
endeavors of man rather than nature.

General:
Tecate is a small, quiet city, close to the U.S. border, but far
enough from San Diego and Calexico that it has not
experienced the popularity, growth and flashiness of Tijuana.
The route provides a variety of Baja scenery from rugged hills
and desert areas to the rich farmlands of the Mexicali Valley.

Point of Entry: Tecate
Tecate is at the junction of two major Baja roads, Highway 2,
connecting Tijuana to Mexicali, and Highway 3, south to
Ensenada and on east to San Felipe. With a population of
34,000 and located at an elevation of 1,620 feet, the town is
primarily an agricultural center for grapes, olives and various
grains.   Vast cattle ranches lie further east.   Foreign
manufacturing is also settling in the area. It is best known,
however, as the producer of Tecate beer. Brewery tours are
conducted the first three Saturdays of each month from 8 a.m.
to 12 noon. Tecate is also famous among cyclists as the start

of the popular Tecate - Ensenada Ride (see "Major Annual Rides," Appendix).

Logistics:
Good bus service exists between San Diego, the major cities of Northern Baja, and Tecate/Mexicali. The bus station is at Av. Benito Juarez and Calle Aberlardo Rodriguez. Services in Tecate include hotels, several restaurants, a wonderful bakery. The Parque Hidalgo, at the junction of Highways 2 and 3, is a pleasant spot from which to view Tecate's passing parade.

Route Log

130 KM; 80.6 Miles (80.6E/ 0.0W; el. 1650 ft.)
Leaving Tecate, a gradual climb begins.

108 KM; 67.0 Miles (67.0E / 13.6W; el. 3100 ft.)
Loncheria and *abarrotes*.

106 KM; 65.7 Miles (65.7E/ 14.9W)
Dirt road to Ojos Negros.

98 KM; 60.8 Miles (60.8E / 19.8W; el. 3300 ft.)
El Hongo - very small town - *abarrotes*.

91 KM; 56.4 Miles (56.4E/ 24.2W)
Some rolling hills for several kilometers - still going up.

82 KM; 50.8 Miles (50.8E/ 29.8W el. 4100 ft.)
El Condor - no services. This is the turn-off for the Laguna Hanson tour (see Tour No. 13).

71 KM; 44.0 Miles (44.0E / 36.6W)
Panaderia La Montana.

69 KM; 42.8 Miles (42.8E/ 37.8W; el. 4200 ft.)
La Rumorosa - a small town with cafe, store and Pemex. The large boulders begin to appear.

65 KM; 40.3 Miles (40.3E / 40.3W)
Begin descending the Cantu Grade - a very curvy drop to the

desert. CAUTION is advised on the open curves due to strong crosswinds.

41 KM; 25.4 Miles (25.4E / 55.2W; el. 700 ft.)
The bottom of the steepest part of the grade, gradual descent from here to sea level. In the far distance you can see clouds above the Cerro Prieto geothermal plant, south of Mexicali. In the foreground is Laguna Salada, which was often a dry lake, dependent upon seasonal rains for water, until a channel was cut from the Rio Hardy at the southern end to fill the basin permanently. You will cross the southern end of the lake on Highway 5 if using the Mexicali - San Felipe route.

29 KM; 18.0 Miles (18.0E / 62.6W)
Dirt road, right to Canon de Guadalupe.

24 KM; 14.9 Miles (14.9E/ 65.7W)
Playa de Laguna Salada - an established campground. Free camping may be found elsewhere around the lake. Very barren countryside. Start 0.5 mile climb.

15 KM; 9.3 Miles (9.3E / 71.3W)
Cultivation starts - no more camping.

10 KM; 6.2 Miles (6.2E / 74.4W)
Housing starts - pop stop.

3 KM; 1.9 Miles (1.9E / 78.7W)
Motel Minols and restaurant.

0.0 KM; 0.0 Miles (0.0E / 80.6W)
If going to downtown Mexicali, continue straight ahead. If going to San Felipe, bear right; this is still Mexico 2 for 4.8 miles.

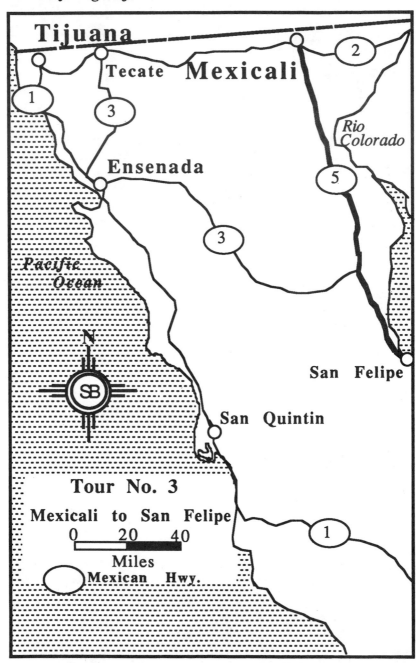

Tijuana

Tecate Mexicali

1

3

Rio Colorado

Ensenada

5

3

Pacific Ocean

N

SB

San Felipe

San Quintin

Tour No. 3

Mexicali to San Felipe

0   20   40

Miles

Mexican Hwy.

1

TOUR NO. 3 - MEXICALI TO SAN FELIPE

Length: 191 KM / 118.4 Miles

Time Required: Two days

Season: Late October to April

Difficulty: Average

Flat, flat, flat with a bump or two, best describes Highway 5 to San Felipe. Long, flat rides can get pretty boring and frequent stops are necessary to relieve the pressure points. The last 30 miles on the arrow-straight, flat road are perhaps the most monotonous, though a little vegetation begins to appear. I've ridden this road several times and the prevailing winds seem to be north to south. Wind velocities can vary, however. On one spring trip the wind was very strong - a great help when trying to make the miles go by quickly.

General:

This is one of the driest desert regions of the entire peninsula with very little vegetation. Fortunately, there is some interesting scenery along the way. The beautiful foothills of San Pedro Martir to the west are in view most of the way, giving way to uninterrupted views of Picacho del Diablo when approaching San Felipe. About 20 miles south of Mexicali you can see the vapor clouds rising from the Cerro Prieto geothermal plants. At about 30 miles south the road parallels the Rio Hardy which provides habitat for a great variety of bird life. Laguna Salada casts lovely pastel colors among its surroundings if crossed in early morning or evening. Then suddenly the sand dunes appear - and just as quickly disappear.

Point of Entry: Mexicali

With a population of 600,000, Mexicali is the capital of the state of Baja California. This city is of major importance to Baja. It is the center of an extremely productive agricultural network. Light manufacturing is another growing industry in this city. Although literally thousands of tourists pass through the border at Mexicali on their way to San Felipe or elsewhere, few stop over here. For those who do there are many points of interest such as lush parks, shopping areas, a civic center with frequent performances and the Mexican rodeos and bullfights.

Much of Mexicali's success is related to the Morelos Dam, on the Colorado River just south of the border. This dam provides the essential water needed by the fertile land.

Logistics:
Good bus service exists between San Diego, Calexico, the major cities of Northern Baja, and Mexicali/San Felipe. Services in Mexicali are plentiful and include several bike shops, motels, and restaurants. If picking up this tour from the border, follow the train tracks along Calzada Lopez Mateos which eventually lead to the junction of Highways 5 and 3. The Mexicali airport has international flight status.

Route Log

0.0 KM; 0.0 Miles (0.0S /118.4N)
Junction of Highways 5 and 2. Highway is a divided 4-lane road with good shoulders.

1.0 KM; 0.6 Miles (0.6S / 117.8N)
Motel El Portal.

18 KM; 11.2 Miles (11.2S / 107.2N)
Road narrows to two lanes and two-way traffic.

19 KM; 11.8 Miles (11.8S / 106.6N)
Pop stop.

20 KM; 12.4 Miles (12.4S/ 106.0 N)
Abarrotes.

22 KM; 13.6 Miles (13.6S / 104.8N)
Road narrows - no shoulders.

23 KM; 14.3 Miles (14.3S / 104.1)
Road right.

25 KM; 15.5 Miles (15.5S / 102.9N)
Road right.

27 KM; 16.7 Miles (16.7S / 101.7N)
Road left.

32 KM; 19.8 Miles (19.8S / 98.6N)
La Puerta. A wide spot in the road with a *farmacia,* restaurant, store. A paved road left leads to the geothermal plant.

50 KM; 31.0 Miles (31.0S / 87.4N)
Road right. Rio Hardy (a tributary of the Colorado River) parallels road for 20 KM.

51 KM; 31.6 Miles (31.6S / 86.8N)
Campo Sonora - camping and restaurant along Rio Hardy. Road widens with good shoulders for a short distance and has water on both sides. Good bird watching area.

56 KM; 34.7 Miles (34.7S / 83.6N)
La Chapparal - pop stop.

67 KM; 41.5 Miles (41.5S / 76.9N)
Road right.

72 KM; 44.6 Miles (44.6S / 73.8N)
Begin raised levee road across Laguna Salada (water on both sides).

87 KM; 53.9 Miles (53.9S / 64.5N)
Roads left and right. Dry lake ends, sand dunes start, road curves and rolls for short distance.

105 KM; 65.1 Miles (65.1S / 53.3N)
La Ventana - meals and Pemex.

109 KM; 67.6 Miles (67.6S / 50.8N)
Road left.

114 KM; 70.7 Miles (70.7S / 47.7N)
Road right.

133 KM; 82.5 Miles (82.5S / 35.9N)
A few ocotillo begin to appear.

140 KM; 86.8 Miles (86.8S / 31.6N)
Rancho - meals.

141 KM; 87.4 Miles (87.4S / 27.4N)
Crucero El Chinero marks the junction of Highways 5 and 3. Crucero El Chinero is a monument to the Chinese immigrants who built the Imperial Canal (1902), which brings water to the rich soil around Mexicali.

142 KM; 88.0 Miles (88.0S / 30.4N)
Pemex station and food available. From this point three "bumps" are visible to the left on the southern horizon. These mark the location of San Felipe.

163 KM; 101.1 Miles (101.1S / 17.3N)
Roads right and left. `More vegetation and ground cover appear. The 4 to 6 foot smoke trees vary in color from dull grey to green. A springtime explosion of violet-blue flowers appears by late April. These trees have a strong fragrance. Small creosote bushes are also seen throughout the area.

169 KM; 104.8 Miles (104.8S / 13.6N)
Road left.

171 KM; 106.0 Miles (106.0S / 12.4N)
Road right. A series of *campos de playas*, to the left, begins here. Some of these are nicely developed campgrounds with electricity and shower facilities, others are nothing more than a road to the beach. Names appear such as: Los Amigos, Playa Grande, Pete's Camp and several unnamed.

178 KM; 110.4 Miles (110.4S / 8.0N)
Sign to **El Saltito**. Col. Morelia dirt road is to the right. This is also the road to Laguna Diablo dry lake at the base of Picacho del Diablo, (10,126 feet), Baja's highest peak.

180 KM; 111.6 Miles (111.6S / 6.8N)
More *campos de playas* :   Campo Hawaii, Pai Pai, San Diego
Beach, Playas del Sol.

184 KM; 114.1 Miles (114.1S / 4.3N)
Rancho with *tortillas* on right.

191 KM; 118.4 Miles (118.4S / 0.0N)
San Felipe. The business area picks up after passing the
large, glimmering, white double arches.

**TOURING EXCHANGE Leader   Brian Rovira watches as
Howard Franklin brings up needed water from a Rancho
well**

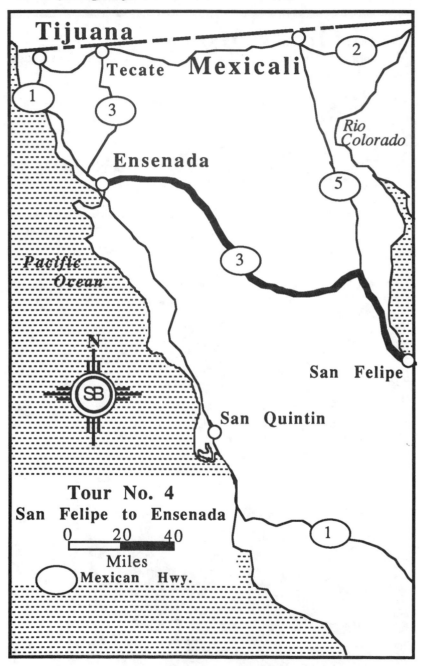

Tijuana

Tecate Mexicali

1

3

Rio Colorado

Ensenada

5

Pacific Ocean

3

N

SB

San Felipe

San Quintin

Tour No. 4
San Felipe to Ensenada
0   20   40
Miles
Mexican Hwy.

1

TOUR NO. 4 - SAN FELIPE TO ENSENADA

Length: 246 KM / 152.5 Miles

Time Required: Three days

Season: September to May. December through
                     February can be cold in the mountains

Difficulty: Average

The first 50 kilometers of this tour are a retracing of Highway 5 (see Tour No. 3) north to the Crucero El Chinero junction. Turning left, or west you are now on Highway 3 traveling west toward Ensenada,   distance, 196 KM.   The road may look level but a gentle climb begins immediately. There is a steep   5 - mile climb past KM155 where the vegetation dramatically changes. Ocotillo, barrel cactus and agave are seen. Out of the canyon, a gentle climb continues and two rich and prosperous valleys, Trinidad and Ojos Negros, are passed through. Both have services but no motels. A long downhill grade returns the route to sea level at the bustling seaport town of Ensenada.

General:

This is a very rewarding tour scenery-wise, and has the least amount of traffic of all the Day-Rides-Near-the-Border tours described herein.

Point of Entry: San Felipe

The main road in San Felipe leads to a traffic circle (turn right for airport and road to Puertecitos) and continues straight to the beach. After the long desert crossing, San Felipe appears as a virtual oasis. However, after a reviving cold drink, a meal and perhaps a *paleta* for dessert, I generally start looking for water, groceries and other supplies in order to be back on the road. It is advisable not to plan a trip to or from San Felipe during American holidays. Motorcycles and three wheelers raise the

the decibel count to a high level. Along Mar de Cortez, where almost everything is in English and civic improvements are made on a regular basis, prosperous merchants are doing a booming business. It is hardly what one calls a "trip to a foreign country" anymore.

Logistics:
This fishing and resort playground thrives on tourist trade and offers most amenities you may be looking for: motels, campgrounds, restaurants, groceries, laundromat, long distance phone, banks which exchange money, medical clinic, good bus service to Mexicali and Ensenada, plenty of beer and liquor stores, post office, bakeries, *tortillerias* and *paleta* shops.   You can buy water at grocery stores in one gallon containers or, where everyone else in town buys water, - at Aqua Pur. It is located next to the Pelicano Mercado y Licores on the corner of Calzada Chetumal and Mar Jonco. Aqua Pur is the white building with blue stripes. You can even buy a shower at a place on the *malecon* (waterfront boardwalk).

Route Log

191 KM; 0.0 Miles (0.0 N / 152.5S)
Leave San Felipe on Highway 5,   and proceed north to Crucero El Chinero junction.

141KM, Highway 5; 196 KM, Highway 3; 31.0 Miles (31.0 N / 121.5S; el. 100 ft.)
Crucero El Chinero.   Junction of Highways 5 and 3. Proceed west on Highway 3.

187 KM; 36.6 Miles (36.6W / 115.9E; el. 800 ft.)
Road right.

181 KM; 40.3 Miles (40.3W / 112.2E)
Road left.

175 KM; 44.0 Miles (44.0W / 108.5E; el. 1300ft.)
Road left.

165 KM; 50.2 Miles (50.2W / 102.3E)
Road left to dry lake bed - **Laguna Diablo.**

155 KM; 56.4 Miles (56.4W / 96.1E; el. 2000 ft.)
Rancho with meals. Start of fairly steep climb.

154 KM; 57.0 Miles (57.0W / 95.5E)
Road left. Ocotillo forest.

146 KM; 62.0 Miles (62.0W / 90.5E; el. 2800 ft.)
Out of the canyon, climb less steep now, rolling hills.

142 KM; 64.5 Miles (64.5W / 88.0E)
San Matias. *Loncheria.*

138 KM; 67.0 Miles (67.0W / 85.5E; el. 2960 ft.)
Road starts gradual descent - still rolling hills. Road left to Mike's Sky Rancho.

137 KM; 67.6 Miles (67.6W / 84.9E)
Small *loncheria.*

136 KM; 68.2 Miles (68.2W / 84.3E)
Irrigated area starts - fences.

130 KM; 71.9 Miles (71.9W / 80.6E)
Campo Christiana - no services. Barrel cactus area.

123 KM; 76.3 Miles (76.3W / 76.2E)
Red Cross station.

121 KM; 77.5 Miles (77.5W / 75.0E; el. 2580 ft.)
Valle la Trinidad - to the left - small farming community with bank, bakery, good *abarrotes* and two cafes for meals. Leaving town, the road starts climbing again.

115 KM; 81.2 Miles (81.2W / 71.3E; el. 3360 ft.)
Summit - road levels off. Rolling terrain - up and down.

110 KM; 84.3 Miles (84.3W / 68.2E)
Road right to **Sonora BFCA** and Laguna Hanson yucca area.

108 KM; 85.6 Miles (85.6W / 66.9E)
Road left.

105 KM; 87.4 Miles (87.4W / 65.1E)
Pop stop.

92 KM; 95.5 Miles (95.5W / 57.0E, el. 3300 ft.)
Ejido Heroes De La Independencia - very small community with cafe, *conosupo* and *tortilleria*.

87KM; 98.6 Miles (98.6W / 53.9E)
Road left to **18 de Marzo**. There are still many fences along this stretch. Some shade trees.

74 KM; 106.6 Miles (106.6W / 45.9E; el. 3560 ft.)
Water available from a pipe along the hillside.

70 KM; 109.1 Miles (109.1W / 43.4E; el. 3900 ft.)
Summit.

59 KM; 115.9 Miles (115.9W / 36.6E)
Road left.

55 KM; 118.4 Miles (118.4W / 34.1E; el. 2800 ft.)
Road right to **Laguna Hanson** - sign says 35 KM.

39 KM; 128.3 Miles (128.3W / 24.2E; el. 2100 ft.)
Ojos Negros. 1.5 miles along a paved road to the right leads to this small farming community. Nice park, *abarrotes,* cafe and campground on the road leading to Laguna Hanson.

38 KM; 129.0 Miles (129.0W / 23.5E)
Start climbing.

35 KM; 130.1 Miles (130.1W / 21.7E; el. 2400 ft.)
Summit.

30 KM; 133.9 Miles (133.9W / 18.6E; el. 1780 ft.)
Bottom of hill. Start climbing.

26 KM; 136.4 Miles (136.4W / 16.1E; 2130 ft.)
Summit.

21 KM; 139.5 Miles (139.5W / 13.0E; el. 1700 ft.).
Bottom of hill. One more short climb.

20 KM; 140.1 Miles (140.1W / 12.4E; el. 1810 ft.)
Pop stop at rancho on right. Summit. Downhill the rest of the
way in to Ensenada.

0.0 KM; 152.5 Miles (152.5W / 0.0E; el. 20 ft.)
Ensenada.

Pacific coastline north of Ensenada, Highway 1

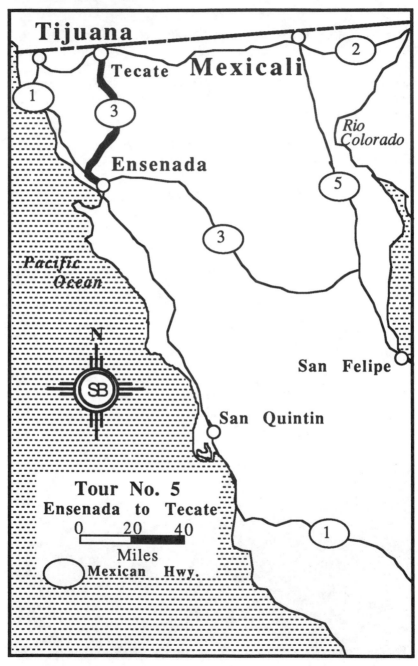

Tour No. 5
Ensenada to Tecate
0   20   40
Miles
Mexican Hwy.

TOUR NO. 5 - ENSENADA TO TECATE

Length: 115 KM / 71.3 Miles

Time Required: One to two days

Season: September to May

Difficulty: Average

The route is generally hilly in nature. It crosses through several valleys separated by hills which have to be climbed before the downhill is enjoyed. As with the San Felipe to Ensenada portion of Highway 3 (Tour No. 4), there is little traffic. However, truck traffic will be encountered as this is the shortest route from Mexicali to the port of Ensenada.

General:

The hilly landscape varies from olive orchards and vineyards near Ensenada, to scrub covered hills near Tecate.

Point of Entry: Ensenada

With 150,000 people, Ensenada is the third largest city in Baja. This Pacific seaside resort town is accessible from San Diego with a two hour drive on the toll road. With weather similar to San Diego, only 10 inches annual rainfall, and cool summer breezes off the bay, the city stays busy all year. Many prefer it to Tijuana for shopping. It has a near constant party atmosphere with cruise ships and boaters calling it a favorite port of call.

Because of its excellent deep water port capabilities, Ensenada is the commercial center for northern Baja's agricultural goods. Fish canneries line Blvd. Azueta. Sportfishing operators flourish along the port docks.

The main strip of tourist hangouts is on Ave. Lopez Mateos. The business district for the locals is along Ave. Juarez and Ave. Ruiz. The famous Hussong's Cantina is located on Ruiz.

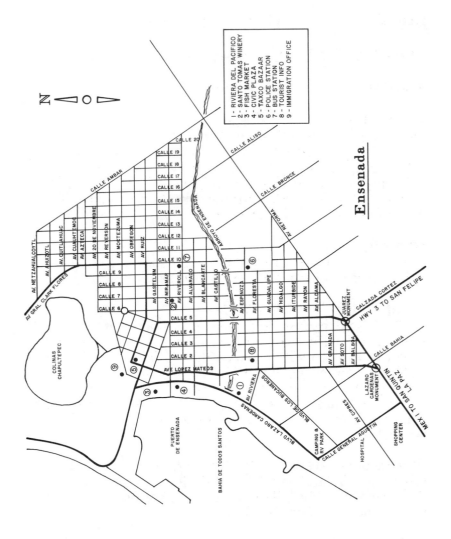

Logistics:

Whatever you forgot to bring you'll be able to find in Ensenada. Several bicycle shops may be found and hotels and restaurants in all price ranges abound. Good bus service exists between San Diego, the major cities of Northern Baja, and Ensenada/Tecate. There are no towns of substantial size between Ensenada and Tecate, but food and drink are available along the route. A reasonable campground is located near 94 KM.

Route Log:

The log starts at the three statues memorial in the Plaza Civica on Blvd. Lazaro Cardenas, Ensenada. Travel will be north on Highway 3.

0.0 Miles (0.0N / 71.7S)
Plaza Civica.

0.4 Miles (0.4N / 71.3S)
Bear left onto Blvd. Azueta and continue on divided road (speed bumps).

1.0 Miles (1.0N / 70.7S)
Road curves right and becomes two lane road with ocean on left.

1.3 Miles (1.3N / 70.4S)
Resume divided roadway.

2.8 Miles (2.8N / 68.9S)
Continue straight past "Highway 1 to San Quintin" sign.

105 KM (KM Post, Highway 3); 6.6 Miles (6.6N / 65.1S)
Bear right onto Highway 3 to Tecate.

103 KM; 7.8 Miles (7.8N / 63.9S)
Picnic table beside the road. Road begins gentle climb.

101 KM; 9.1 Miles (9.1N / 62.6S)
Climb steepens. Both sides of road are cultivated and/or fenced.

99 KM; 10.3 Miles (10.3N / 61.4S)
Summit.

97 KM; 11.6 Miles (11.6N / 60.1S)
Rolling hills.

96 KM; 12.2 Miles (12.2N / 59.5S)
Picnic table.

95 KM; 12.8 Miles (12.8N / 58.9S)
Abarrotes. Rolling hills continue.

94 KM; 13.4 Miles (13.4N / 58.3S)
Camping area among oak trees and next to rancho.

77 KM; 24.0 Miles (24.0N / 47.7S)
Mercado. Turnoff for Valle de GPE (Guadalupe). Town is of Russian descent though no Russians remain. Guadalupe is also the site of the last mission established in Baja during the mission movement (1834 -1840).

76 KM; 24.6 Miles (24.6N / 47.1S)
Top of hill, short descent then a gradual climb.

73 KM; 26.4 Miles (26.4N / 45.3S)
Domecq Winery - not open for tours.

67 KM; 30.2 Miles (30.2N / 41.5S)
Steeper climb.

63 KM; 32.6 Miles (32.6N / 39.1S)
Pop stop - followed by top of hill.

60 KM; 34.5 Miles (34.5N / 37.2S).
Road levels off.

55 KM; 37.6 Miles (37.6N / 34.1S)
Climb.

49 KM; 41.3 Miles (41.3N / 30.4S).
El Testerazo - pop stop, cafe, store.

47 KM; 42.6 Miles (42.6N / 29.1S).
Climb.

41 KM; 46.3 Miles (46.3N / 25.4S).
Summit.

29 KM; 53.7 Miles (53.7N / 18.0 S)
Valle las Palmas - cafes, Pemex, *mercado*.

27 KM; 55.0 Miles (55.0 N / 16.7S).
Uphill stretch. Rolling hills.

15 KM; 62.4 Miles (62.4N / 9.3S)
Summit.

14 KM; 63.0 Miles (63.0 N / 8.7S)
Abarrotes.

4 KM; 69.2 Miles (69.2 N/ 2.5S)
Road continues downhill.   550 meters elevation (1804 feet),
per road sign.

2 KM; 70.5 Miles (70.5N / 1.2S)
Fonart appears on right just before the bridge and the railroad
tracks. Arts and crafts for sale here, when open.

0.0 KM; 71.7 Miles (71.7N / 0.0S)
Tecate.

TRANSPENINSULAR TOURS

This section consists of seven tours which may be taken individually, in combinations, or as one long chain down the full length of the Baja peninsula, from Tijuana to Cabo San Lucas. By employing public transportation to the points of entry or destination, it becomes possible to take an individual tour or a limited combination of tours. Tour No. 1 "Tijuana to Ensenada" is described in the section "Day Tours Near the Border." It may be included in the chain from the U.S. border to Cabo San Lucas, or in combinations of tours. The Transpeninsular Tours, described in this section, are listed below:

Tour No. 6 - Ensenada to San Quintin

Tour No. 7 - San Quintin to Guerrero Negro

Tour No. 8 - Guerrero Negro to Santa Rosalia

Tour No. 9 - Santa Rosalia to Loreto

Tour No. 10 - Loreto to La Paz

Tour No. 11 - La Paz to Cabo San Lucas Via Highway 1

Tour No. 12 - La Paz to Cabo San Lucas Via Highway 19

Giant cardon cactus in bloom (white flowers); dirt road near Catavina

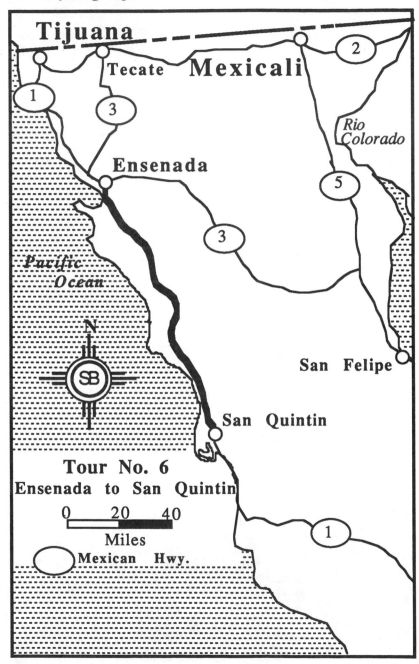

Tijuana

Tecate   Mexicali

1

3

Rio
Colorado

Ensenada

5

3

Pacific
Ocean

N

San Felipe

San Quintin

Tour No. 6
Ensenada to San Quintin

0   20   40
Miles
Mexican Hwy.

1

TOUR NO. 6 - ENSENADA TO SAN QUINTIN

Length: 198 KM / 121 Miles

Time Required: Two to three days

Season: September to May

Difficulty: Average

The road to Maneadero is fairly flat. It is followed by curved road and low, rolling hills near Santo Tomas. From the fine vista point of the valley, there is a good downhill with switchbacks. This is followed by a flat ride across the valley and a 5 KM ascent leaving the valley. From there, it is rolling hills with two 2 KM climbs and a flat stretch into Colonet. Though this latter stretch of road is not totally flat, it is an easy ride in to San Quintin.

General:

This whole section has changed rapidly and quite drastically in the last 5 years. There used to be mile upon mile of open desert and camping was unlimited. By drilling deep wells into "fossil water" (underground prehistoric lakes) the desert area is literally blooming with various crops and the population centers are all growing.

Point of Entry: Ensenada

Ensenada is the third largest city in Baja. It is a very active seaport as well as a trade center. Services available are more than ample. See Tour No. 5 for a more detailed description of Ensenada.

Logistics:

Ensenada and San Quintin may be reached by bus from the major cities of Baja. Ensenada has most of the services needed by any bicycle tourist (See Tour No. 1).

Services at San Quintin are not as varied as in Ensenada, but are good.

The growth in agriculture and population in this area of Baja has two direct effects on the cyclist. First of all, campsites aren't as frequent as they used to be. Please respect fences and crops and ask for permission at a rancho to camp. Read the road log carefully and plan your rides through this section with care. Secondly, more people mean more services and also more traffic, though traffic is still considered light after Maneadero. More frequent services mean you don't have to haul food and water for long distances, as in the old days.

Route Log

Distances are entered in miles from Ensenada to Maneadero.

0.0 Miles (0.0S / 120.9N; el. 10 ft.)
Start tour at the Plaza Civica with its memorial statues of three heads of Mexican leaders.

1.6 Miles (1.6S / 119.3N; el. 30 ft.)
Right at top of small hill past hospital - there's a sign "Estero Beach." This is Mexico 1, but there's no sign saying so. This is a good corner for shopping. A bank is across the street, shopping center with supermarket on right, *panaderia* next to the market and another one across the street.

2.6 Miles (2.6S / 118.3N)
Tortilleria and *pan* on left.

3.0 Miles (3.0S / 117.9N)
Fruit stand on right.

4.7 Miles (4.7S / 116.2N)
Paleteria and *abarrotes* on right.

5.0 Miles (5.0S / 115.9N)
Campo de Militar.

6.6 Miles (6.6S / 114.3N)
Estero Beach turn-off to right, RV park and motel on the beach. *Tortilleria* and restaurant also on this corner.

11.1 Miles (11.1S / 109.8N; el. 60 ft.)
Maneadero - pop. 30,000. This is the farthest south into Baja that you can go without a tourist permit. The checkpoint station reopened here in 1986 and you need to stop here and get your tourist card validated. Remember to have your identification with you. The community is a fast-growing agricultural center with few tourist services, although there is a small motel, and places to eat or buy groceries. From here on the kilometer posts along the side of the road are consistently placed. This road log, from Maneadero on, includes distances in kilometers as read from these kilometer posts.

24 KM; 14.0 Miles (14.0S / 106.9N)
Los Arcos Motel and restaurant in **Maneadero.** Few rolling hills south of town. Maximum elevation, 500 feet.

41 KM; 24.5 Miles (24.5S / 96.4N)
Sign for campground to the left.

43 KM; 25.8 Miles (25.8S / 95.1; el. 680 ft.)
Start climb.

45 KM; 27.0 Miles (27.0S / 93.9N; el. 1000 ft.)
Top - good view of the Santo Tomas Valley.

51 KM; 30.7 Miles (30.7S / 90.2N; el. 540 ft.)
Santo Tomas - small village, dating back to the mission days. Consists of several houses clustered alongside the road. Town is well known for its grape producing valley and its wine. However, the winery is now located in Ensenada (see "Excursions," Appendix). Olive trees are more prevalent now. El Palomar Motel, campground, general store (limited groceries) and Red Cross clinic are available.

58 KM; 35.1 Miles (35.1S / 85.8N; el. 700 ft.)
Start climb.

63 KM; 38.2 Miles (38.2S / 82.7N; el. 1520 ft.)
Summit.

68 KM; 41.3 Miles (41.3S / 79.6N)
Road right to *ejido*.

79 KM; 48.1 Miles (48.1S / 72.8N; el. 500 ft.)
Paved road to **Ejido Erendira** - start climb.

81 KM; 49.3 Miles (49.3S / 71.6N; el. 850 ft.)
Summit.

89 KM; 54.3 Miles (54.3S / 66.6N; el. 380 ft.)
San Vincente - pop. 6,000.   Started in 1780 as a Dominican
Mission site, San Vincente fell into collapse and didn't revive
until   the   1940s.   Rejuvenation   was   brought   about   by
agricultural development.   Services include: Cafe Colonial,
nice plaza on right (water), *abarrotes, panaderia,* and Motel El
Camino.   Emergency radio communication - ask for Queta
McFarland at the cafe.

92 KM; 56.2 Miles (56.2S / 64.7N)
Road left - another road soon after.

93 KM; 56.8 Miles (56.8S / 64.1N)
Road left.

95 KM; 58.0 Miles (58.0S/ 62.9N)
Ejido Toboda - no services except *Abarrotes* San Miguel.

96 KM; 58.6 Miles (58.6S / 62.3N)
Abarrotes Sanchez.

97 KM; 59.3 Miles (59.3S / 61.6N)
Road left - camping by the rocks.

102 KM; 62.4 Miles (62.4S / 58.5N)
Road left to Los Coches.

105 KM; 64.2 Miles (64.2S / 56.7N)
Ejido Guadalupe and Isabel.

108 KM; 66.1 Miles (66.1S / 54.8N; el. 320 ft.)
Start climb.

111 KM; 67.9 Miles (67.9S / 53.0N; el. 710 ft.)
Summit.

116 KM; 71.0 Miles (71.0S / 49.9N)
Bottom of hill, road heads west. There is almost always a headwind until Colonet. *Abarrotes.*

118 KM; 72.3 Miles (72.3S / 48.6N)
Road left to **Ejido Morales.**

121 KM; 74.1 Miles (74.1S / 46.8N)
Ejido Lopez Aomora.

123 KM; 75.4 Miles (75.4S / 45.5N)
Panaderia Carmen on right.

126 KM; 77.2 Miles (77.2S / 43.7N)
Road right to San Antonio de Mar (on the coast). Highway 1 also swings south again and hopefully a tailwind is back!

127 KM; 77.9 Miles (77.9S / 43.0 N; el. 160 ft.)
Colonet - pop. 2,000. It's not unusual to have school kids in the road flagging traffic to stop. They then solicit a contribution for the Red Cross. For any amount of loose change you drop in the tin you'll get some sort of sticker to show your participation. Attach this to your bicycle in plain sight to show the next group collecting money that you've already donated. Of course, a handful of pesos at each stop wouldn't hurt either. I find it's a good way to get rid of the heavy coins that don't buy much anywhere else. Here it gets a huge smile and happy *"Gracias!" Panaderia, abarrotes, loncheria.*

130 KM; 79.7 Miles (79.7S / 41.2N)
Road left to **Ejido Benito Juarez.**

131 KM; 80.3 Miles (80.3S / 40.6N)
Road right.

138 KM; 84.7 Miles (84.7S / 36.2N; el. 200 ft.)
Ejido Hereos de Chultepec - no services yet.

140 KM; 85.9 Miles (85.9S / 35.0N; el. 130 ft.)
Ejido Ordaz - *conosupo*. Nearby is the turnoff for San Telmo, 6 miles, the Meling Rancho, high in the mountains at 31 miles, and the National Observatory atop Picacho del Diablo, elevation 10,126 feet, some 60 miles away.

144 KM; 88.4 Miles (88.4S / 32.5N)
Road right - open fields.

146 KM; 89.6 Miles (89.6S / 31.3N; el. 130 ft.)
Ejido Rueban Jaramillo - pop stop, *correo*.

151 KM; 92.7 Miles (92.7S / 28.2N)
Road left.

152 KM; 93.4 Miles (93.4S / 27.5N; el. 340 ft.)
Top of short hill.

153 KM; 94.0 Miles (94.0S / 26.9N)
Road right.

156 KM; 95.8 Miles (95.8S / 25.1N; el. 160 ft.)
Camalu - very small town spread alongside the highway. It has open air market day with several traveling merchants, on Mondays. *Conosupo, correo*, Red Cross, ABC bus stop, pop stops, telephone service, taco stands, *loncheria, cerveza deposito*.

165 KM; 101.4 Miles (101.4S / 19.5N)
Road left.

166 KM; 102.0 Miles (102.0S / 18.9N; el. 140 ft.)
Ejido Emiliano Zapata - *conosupo, abarrotes*.

169 KM; 103.9 Miles (103.9S / 17.0 N)
Road left to Mission Santo Domingo.

171 KM; 105.1 Miles (105.1S / 15.8N; el.110 ft.)
Colonia Vicente Guerrero - another fast-growing agricultural community. Fields of chile peppers, cauliflower, brussel sprouts, tomatoes and grains are seen throughout the region. The same open market of Camalu is also here on Tuesdays. Bank, hospital, several grocery stores, telegraph office, Motel Sanchez, Restaurant Vera Cruz.

173 KM; 106.4 Miles (106.4S / 14.5N)
Right turn for two trailer parks with camping (hot showers and laundry) - Don Diego and Don Pepe. Both have restaurants. Cafe Nuevo.

174 KM; 107.0 Miles (107.0S / 13.9N)
Road left.

175 KM; 107.6 Miles (107.6S / 13.3N)
Road right.

178 KM; 109.5 Miles (109.5S / 11.4N)
Factory on left.

179 KM; 110.1 Miles (110.1S / 10.8N)
Conosupo on left.

189 KM; 116.3 Miles (116.3S / 4.6N; el. 80 ft.)
Approaching **San Quintin.**

198 KM; 120.9 Miles (120.9S / 0.0N; el. 120 ft.)
End of **San Quintin** development.

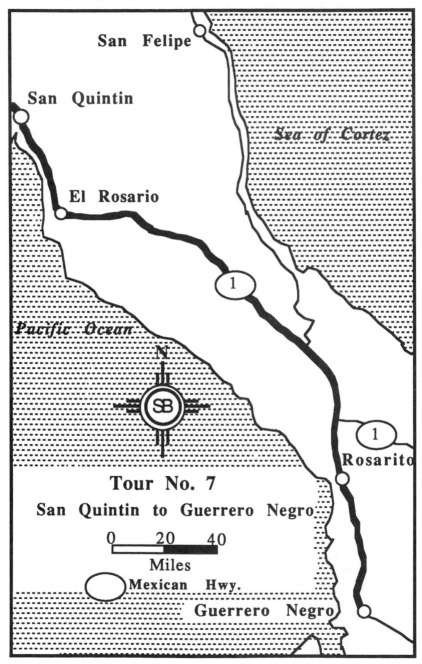

San Felipe

San Quintin

Sea of Cortez

El Rosario

1

Pacific Ocean

N

SB

1

Rosarito

Tour No. 7

San Quintin to Guerrero Negro

0   20   40
Miles

Mexican Hwy.

Guerrero Negro

TOUR NO. 7 - SAN QUINTIN TO GUERRERO NEGRO

Length: 408 KM / 253 Miles

Time Required: Five to seven days

Season: October to April

Difficulty: Average

The ride to El Rosario has some rolling hills parallel to the coastline with fine ocean views most of the way. There is a steep, three kilometer climb to a mesa top then a steep descent into El Rosario. After leaving the wide arroyo containing the town, there are some 40 kilometers of ups and downs, mostly up. After the hills, the road continues to the "Big Rocks," or "Rock Garden" of Catavina. The area is designated as a natural preserve by the government and should not be passed through too quickly. It is a highlight of the northern half of the peninsula.

The climbs that follow take you to the highest point on the Transpeninsular Highway. Soon after, one sees the expansive dry lake bed of Laguna Chapala. I've seen this filled with water twice after heavy rains and it is a magnificent sight. After one more short hill, it is a good, fast ride to the Punta Prieta Junction. Here the paved 45 mile road to Bahia de Los Angeles on the Sea of Cortez turns off. South of this junction there are no major climbs. However, the road becomes very narrow and is often in poor repair close to Guerrero Negro.

General:

The real Baja desert area asserts itself as you leave San Quintin, El Rosario, the string of Pacific coast agricultural towns and the coast itself behind. This part of the ride will either captivate you or find you head down and anxious to reach civilization again. The area abounds in Baja desert vegetation - cirios, ocotillo, cardon, elephant trees, yucca, etc. - and what seem to be, the ever-present hills.

The route south of the junction with the Bahia de Los Angeles road is, to me, the most boring stretch on the peninsula. I'm always glad to finally reach Guerrero Negro, though it is no prize for scenic beauty or cleanliness. The vegetation suddenly drops off to absolutely nothing for mile upon mile.

Point of Entry: San Quintin

This sprawling town of 15,000 is the major center for the bustling agricultural industry of the area. Strip development is prevalent here and stretches out over nearly 10 kilometers. San Quintin is also a popular resort area without the Ensenada-type glitz. Many retirement groups find their way to Bahia San Quintin and the Pacific beaches south of town off Highway 1. Many like the close proximity to the border, but the weather isn't going to be that much different than in San Diego. Most businesses are located in the northern section and start after the first Pemex, which also features good fruit cups from the cart vendor.

There is a large factory on the left as you enter town from the north.   Streams of bicyclists will pour from the gates around quitting time. This is the one town in Baja where I've seen lots of Mexicans riding bikes. The bicycle shop on the right has been there as far back as my first long peninsula tour of 1974.   A public open market is held every Saturday and Sunday where open stalls are filled with consumer goods, especially clothes and radio equipment. There are lots of food stalls, of course.   The homemade potato chips are worth a stop. The market has two locations, both on the left. A few blocks of business buildings separate them starting after the Pemex station.

Logistics:

Bus service to San Quintin and El Rosario from the major cities of Northern Baja is available. San Quintin features full services including supermarkets, cafes, bank, telephone, *tortilleria, panaderia*. Motel Chavez is very clean and quite reasonable. At least two bike shops, a new medical clinic in the second section, and a huge supermarket are found just after the *campo militar* on the right.   Showers (banos) can be purchased in this section also. A very nice restaurant on the left is past the Pemex. About 1-1/2 miles past the second business section is a dirt road right for 3-1/2 miles to the Bay of San Quintin and two motels.

From El Rosario, it is a long 356 kilometers to the next town of Guerrero Negro. This stretch is where the small ranchos serve as the cyclists lifeline to make the crossing possible with food and water. Groceries, however, need to be purchased in El Rosario. Rainfall here averages only 5 inches annually. Services at El Rosario include 2 markets, 3 cafes, a meager *panaderia*, Motel Rosario and several beer stands, a *militar* and SCT *campamento*.

Services at the junction with the Bahia de los Angeles road are very limited. Services along the route from the junction to Guerrero Negro are few. Most services necessary to a cyclist however, are available in Guerrero Negro. Bus service from Guerrero Negro to the major cities of Baja is available. The barrenness of the area along this route and typical strong winds do not provide much protection for camping. There are more and more long stretches of fence appearing.

Route Log:
The route starts at the end of the San Quintin development. The kilometer readings shown refer to those shown on kilometer posts along the route. Note: the kilometer posts are renumbered in ascending order from the Bahia de los Angeles junction south to Guerrero Negro.

0.0 Miles (0.0S / 253.0 N)
Leaving **San Quintin.**

3 KM; 1.9 Miles (1.9S / 251.2N)
Road right to Old Mill Motel on the bay. Dirt road.

5 KM; 3.1 Miles (3.1S / 249.9N; el. 150 ft.)
Left at the Y - both roads will go south to El Rosario. The sign will direct you to the left road, however, and this log follows that road.

11 KM; 6.8 Miles (6.8S / 246.2N)
Cielito Lindo (motel and campground) and La Pinta Hotel turnoff - 3 KM.

13 KM; 8.1 Miles (8.1S / 244.9N)
Paved road right to **Santa Maria.**

14 KM; 8.7 Miles (8.7S / 244.3N)
Old road merges from the right.

16 KM; 9.9 Miles (9.9S / 243.1N; el. 100 ft.)
Sign for Honey's RV park to the right one mile away and on the beach. Cheese sold in roadside *tienda*.

20 KM; 12.4 Miles (12.4S / 240.6N)
Ocean views, rolling hills, fenced agricultural fields.

26 KM; 16.1 Miles (16.1S / 236.4N)
For the next 14 KM several dirt roads lead to the beach. There are some short distances for beach camping, no facilities. It's usually windy along here with lots of dew at night, if no wind.

28 KM; 17.4 Miles (17.4S / 235.6N)
House on right with *"Conosupo"* sign and table outside.

40 KM; 24.8 Miles (24.8S / 228.2N; el. 80 ft.)
Last beach access - road turns inland.

42 KM; 26.0 Miles (26.0S / 227.0 N; el. 110 ft.)
Road right.

46 KM; 28.5 Miles (28.5S / 224.5; el. 320 ft.)
Road left.

48 KM; 29.8 Miles (29.8S/ 223.2N; el. 480 ft.)
Start climb.

49 KM; 30.4 Miles (30.4S / 222.6N; el. 880 ft.)
Summit.

55 KM; 34.1 Miles (34.1S / 218.9N; el. 110 ft.)
El Rosario - long considered the "last outpost of civilization" before the pavement continued beyond this small fishing and agricultural town. In the early days of the Baja 1000 road race it was also a favorite stopping spot, primarily because of the

Espinosa   family   who ran a cafe and motel.   Heraclio
Espinosa, a real pioneer of the area, died in 1985 and many oldtime Baja buffs were saddened with his passing.   Dona Anita
and other family members still run the restaurant and give
advice to those adventurous bicyclists who still consider El
Rosario a "last outpost."

62 KM; 38.4 Miles (38.4S / 214.6; el. 260 ft.)
New bridge - as with many of the nice new bridges you've
crossed since Tijuana, these are substantial and high enough to
hopefully not be washed away with every severe winter storm,
as in the past.   By now you've adjusted to the routine of
touring and have strengthened your cycling muscles. The next
40 kilometers will definitely give you a workout. It is not all
an upward push, but rather up a lot and down a little, up a little
higher and down a little, etc. The highest elevation of the hills
is reached at 1900 feet.   Finding a flat spot off the road for
camping is tough, so you should plan to do this in one stretch
if you can.

63 KM; 39.1 Miles (39.1S / 213.9N; el. 280 ft.)
Start climbing.

66 KM; 40.9 Miles (40.9S / 212.1N; el. 520 ft.)
A summit. Ocotillo cacti begin to appear. This colorful plant
is easy to recognize. There is no main trunk but rather many
long wands fanning out from the base. The branches are
covered with thorns and with sufficient rain, or ocean
moisture, bright green leaves cover the sometimes not so
straight wands. Also with the water come bright red flowers,
the ends of which attract hummingbirds, and make good close-
up photos against a blue sky.

67 KM; 41.5 Miles (41.5S / 211.5N; el. 490 ft.)
Uphill again.

69 KM; 42.8 Miles (42.8S / 210.2N; el. 640 ft.)
Summit. Boojums begin to appear. The cirio tree is popularly
known as "boojum" from Lewis Carroll's desert creature in
"The Hunting of the Snark." Some botanist made this
connection (somehow) and the name boojum and cirio are

synonymous. Without a doubt it is the most unmistakable plant on the peninsula and indigenous only to Baja. Characterized as the upside down carrot, the tall, tapering trunk often sprouts numerous twisting, turning, bizarre shaped stems at the top. At the tips are creamy white or yellow blossoms when enough water. When there's not enough water the plant doesn't grow but produces a thick, waxy covering to prevent loss of moisture. You'll see lots of different shapes on these plants as far south as Guerrero Negro.

71 KM; 44.0 Miles (44S / 209.2N)
Levels.

Mary Sinclair stops to take a picture of ocotillo, which has a flaming red flower when blooming

73 KM; 45.3 Miles (45.3S / 207.7N; el. 620 ft.)
Uphill.

76 KM; 47.1 Miles (47.1S / 205.9N; el. 1020 ft.)
A summit - road right to **Ejido Rodriguez.**

78 KM; 48.4 Miles (48.4S / 204.6N; el. 1000 ft.)
Down.

79 KM; 49.0 Miles (49.0S / 204.0 N; el. 980 ft.)
Road right at bottom of dip.

80 KM; 49.6 Miles (49.6S / 203.4N; el. 900 ft.)
Uphill.

82 KM; 50.8 Miles (50.8S / 202.2N; el. 1360 ft.)
A summit.

87 KM; 53.9 Miles (53.9S / 199.1N; el. 1460 ft.)
Uphill.

88 KM; 54.6 Miles (54.6S / 198.4 N)
Uphill.

89 KM; 55.2 Miles (55.2S / 197.8N)
A summit.

90 KM; 55.8 Miles (55.8S / 197.2N; el. 1900 ft.)
The summit.

92 KM; 57.0 Miles (57.0S / 196.0N; el. 1580 ft.)
This is the steepest downhill.

94 KM; 58.3 Miles (58.3S / 194.7N; el. 1620 ft.)
Rolling hills.

96 KM; 59.5 Miles (59.5S/ 193.5N)
Most of down done.

99 KM; 61.4 Miles (61.4S / 191.6N; el.1750 ft.)
Road left to Los Martires.

103 KM; 63.9 Miles (63.9S / 189.1N)
Road left.

104 KM; 64.5 Miles (64.5S / 188.5N)
Road levels out - still in rolling hills.   Other prominent Baja cacti have begun to appear in this section, namely the cardon, often mistaken as the Arizona saguaro.   As another cactus found only in Baja, the cardon is a very large columnar tree with one main trunk and several huge limbs growing upward. These sentinels of the desert provide beautiful backdrops for sunrise or sunset photos. A dozen or so ribs make up the main trunk to support the tremendous weight of the arms. A dead cardon provides good firewood.   In the spring you may see brown fuzzy balls toward the top of the arms.   Later these burst open into white, fragrant flowers. I've seen the flowers as early as March on the cape loop and in April in the San Ignacio area. The larger cardons can be 60 years old.

Tinker Rovira in tent; giant cardon in background

114 KM; 70.7 Miles (70.7S / 182.3N; el. 1800 ft.)
Dirt road right to **Mission San Fernando** ruins (3 mi.).

116 KM; 71.9 Miles (71.9S / 181.1N)
Rancho El Progreso - pop stop and (sometimes) meals.

118 KM; 73.2 Miles (73.2S / 179.8N)
Rancho Cecilia - well.

119 KM; 73.8 Miles (73.8S / 179.2N; el. 1760 ft.)
Uphill.

120 KM; 74.4 Miles (74.4S / 178.6N; el. 1820 ft.)
Summit - road right.

122 KM; 75.6 Miles (75.6S / 177.4N)
Road right.

123 KM; 76.3 Miles (76.3S / 176.7N; el. 1800 ft.)
Pink cafe on left.

127 KM; 78.7 Miles (78.7S / 174.3N; el. 1900 ft.)
Road right to **Puerto Santa Catarina**, 33 KM. Also a road left, 1 KM to **Guayquil** (sign says *comida* and soda) and it's down a hill.

134 KM; 83.1 Miles (83.1S / 169.9N)
Datilillo appear. These are often referred to as Joshua trees by those familiar with the U.S. Southwest desert. They can be 10 to 20 feet high and branch out from anywhere along the trunk. The leaves are long, narrow, stiff and sharp. You can see these along the road here and there all the way to the cape.

136 KM; 84.3 Miles (84.3S / 168.7N; el. 1960 ft.)
Road left to **Valle Santa Teresa**.

140 KM; 86.8 Miles (86.8S / 166.2N; el. 2000 ft.)
San Agustin - abandoned and locked trailer park. Can usually get meals at **Rancho Guille** on the left. There's also an SCT *campamento*.

141 KM; 87.4 Miles (87.4S / 165.6N)
Road right.

142 KM; 88.0 Miles (88.0S / 165.0 N)
Road left.

143 KM; 88.7 Miles (88.7S / 164.3N; el. 2020 ft.)
Tres Enriques cafe - clean, tidy and good meals.   Ocotillo
appear.

144 KM; 89.3 Miles (89.3S / 163.7N)
Road left to **El Marmol** 15 KM.

158 KM; 98.0 Miles (98S / 155.0 N)
Starting the Big Rocks.   There are huge boulders strewn
across the landscape all the way to the Sea of Cortez in a
southeasterly direction.   It is a fascinating area with small
spring fed pools of water and some palms dotting the two
arroyos which cross the road.   It is highly recommended you
plan your day to allow some time to explore here or, best of
all, camp for the night - there's also an abundance of wildlife.
Food and water are nearby.   Besides the now familiar
boojums, ocotillo and cardons you'll also see another unusual
Baja tree, the torote, more commonly known as the elephant
tree.   A short and thick tree, it doesn't look very well-
proportioned but its survival in such a harsh environment has
been accomplished by its adaptations.   There are many
branches spreading out covered with green leaves that turn
yellow in a dry period or may drop completely; small white
flowers bloom in summer. The thick trunk stores water and
the light   papery bark peels off in yellowish or white
sheets.

160 KM; 99.2 Miles (99.2S / 153.8N)
Camp may be set up on any of the side roads and used as a
base from which to explore this great area.

162 KM; 100.4 Miles (100.4S / 152.6N)
Road right to San Jose on the Pacific coast.

171 KM; 106.0 Miles (106.0S / 147.0 N)
Spring water and palms in *vado*. A short distance up the arroyo to the left is a series of pools which can be refreshing and, if camping, a good place to watch for evening wildlife. Also up this arroyo and shortly after the pools are some cave paintings. These are very small in scale and perhaps not nearly as old or as impressive as some, but worth a look.

174 KM; 108.0 Miles (108.0S / 145.1N; el. 180 ft.)
Catavina - not a town, but it does have what a cyclist needs - a La Pinta Hotel (water from the outside faucet is good), an RV trailer park which sometimes has hot showers, cafe (La Enramada next to the Pemex), and a small grocery.

175 KM; 108.5 Miles (108.5S / 144.5 N)
Spring and palms in *vado*. Santa Ines Rancho turn-off- 1 KM to the left on   paved road. This is another oldtime landmark of the Baja 1000 race days. Besides the cafe, there are some very plain rooms for rent.   The cafe does have some old favorites like hot cakes or French toast, if you're tired of beans by now.   To me the cafe has lost some of the Mexican flavor. The last time I ate there they didn't even serve tortillas with the dinner! Lots of Americans eat here and they now seem to focus on fritos and tacos.

180 KM; 111.6 Miles (111.6S / 141.4 N)
Big rocks end.

185 KM; 114.7 Miles (114.7S / 138.3N)
Road right.

186 KM; 115.3 Miles (115.3S / 137.7N)
Rancho with good food.

188 KM; 116.6 Miles (116.6S / 136.4 N)
Few more of the big rocks.

189 KM; 117.2 Miles (117.2S / 135.8N)
Road right.

---

192 KM; 119.0 Miles(119.0S / 134.0N; el. 2380ft.)
Start climb.

195 KM; 120.9 Miles(120.9S / 132.1N; el. 2880ft.)
Summit - highest point on Highway 1!

206 KM; 127.7 Miles(127.7S / 125.3N; el. 2540ft.)
El Pedegrosa - a big pile of rocks, cone shaped, on a very flat plain, no vegetation, no services.

209 KM; 129.6 Miles(129.6S / 123.4N; el. 2540ft.)
Start climb.

211 KM; 130.8 Miles(130.8S / 122.2N; el. 2710ft.)
Summit.

226 KM; 140.1 Miles (140.1S / 112.9N)
Road left.

230 KM; 142.6 Miles (142.6S / 110.4N)
Road left to **Bahia San Luis Gonzaga** (see "Rough Stuff, Off-Highway Tours"). Road sign here says: **Calamajue 60 KM.**

231 KM; 143.2 Miles(143.2S / 109.8N; el. 2120ft.)
Rancho Chapala - good meals.

238 KM; 147.6 Miles(147.6S / 105.4N; el. 2180ft.)
Start climb.

239 KM; 148.2 Miles(148.2S / 104.8N; el. 2340ft.)
Summit.

240 KM; 148.8 Miles(148.8S / 104.2N; el. 2200ft.)
Nice cardon forest, called a cardonal.

241 KM; 149.4 Miles (149.4S / 103.6N)
More big rocks for next 3 KM.

254 KM; 157.5 Miles (157.5S / 95.5N)
Lots of yuccas appear.

258 KM; 160.0 Miles (160.0S / 93.0 N)
Road left to **Bahia Gonzaga** and **San Felipe** by way of
Calamajue Canyon.

267 KM; 165.5 Miles (165.5S / 87.5N)
Road left - good cactus garden area.

280 KM; 173.6 Miles (173.6S / 79.4N; el. 1130 ft.)
Junction with road to **Bahia de los Angeles** - 42 miles of
rough, paved road.

**Mary Sinclair with one of the mysteries of nature: a
boojum growing from a giant boulder**

0 KM; 173.6 Miles (173.6S· / 79.4N)
This part of the tour begins at the junction with the **Bahia de Los Angeles** road. Note that the kilometer posts are renumbered in ascending order from the **Bahia de Los Angeles** junction south to **Guerrero Negro.**

5 KM; 176.7 Miles (176.7S / 76.3N)
Road right.

10 KM; 179.8 Miles (179.8S / 73.2N)
Road left.

13 KM; 181.7 Miles (181.7S / 71.3N; el. 660 ft.)
Punta Prieta junction - a small village off 1 KM to the right. *Prieta* means dark, thus the name means dark point. At the junction is a *loncheria*, school and SCT *campamento.*

24 KM; 188.5 Miles (188.5S / 64.5N; el. 480 ft.)
Roads right and left. Start climb.

29 KM; 191.6 Miles (191.6 S / 61.4N; el. 830 ft.)
Summit.

32 KM; 193.4 Miles (193.4S / 59.6N)
Roads right.

33 KM; 194.1Miles (194.1S / 58.9N)
Roads right.

38 KM; 197.2 Miles (197.2S / 55.8N)
Roads right.

49 KM; 204.0 Miles (204.0S / 49.0 N)
Roads right.

51 KM; 205.2 Miles (205.2S / 47.8N; el. 300 ft.)
Rosarito - small village - abandoned RV park, *conosupo*, two *loncherias.*

57 KM; 208.9 Miles (208.9S / 44.1N)
Road left.

68 KM; 215.8 Miles (215.8S / 37.2N)
Road right to **El Tomatal** - three miles to a palm-shrouded camping spot close to the beach.

71 KM; 217.6 Miles (217.6 S / 35.4N)
Road right.

73 KM; 218.9 Miles (218.9S / 34.1N)
Road left.

80 KM; 223.2 Miles (223.2S / 29.8N)
Fences on both sides of the road for the next few kilometers.

90 KM; 229.4 Miles (229.4S / 23.6N)
Rancho Experanza - good meals.

95 KM; 232.5 Miles (232.5S / 20.5N; el. 80 ft.)
Ejido Jesus Maria - though not a town, it's only a matter of time as this small cluster of homes has grown rapidly. *Conosupo* and *loncheria*, drinking water at the Pemex.

96 KM; 233.1 Miles 233.1S / 19.9N)
Road right to **Ejido Moreles**, 3 KM, **Laguna Manuela**, 12KM. Pavement stops after a mile. No more cactus - very barren and more fence on the left.

101 KM; 236.2 Miles (236.2S / 16.8N)
Roads right.

102 KM; 236.8 Miles (236.8S / 16.2N)
Roads right.

106 KM; 239.3 Miles (239.3S / 13.7N)
Roads right.

111 KM; 242.4 Miles (242.4S / 10.6N)
Road left.

118 KM; 246.8Miles (246.8S / 6.2N)
Road right.

---

119 KM; 247.4 Miles (247.4S / 5.6N)
Fence ends.

120 KM; 248.0 Miles (248.0S / 5.0N)
Eagle monument begins to appear on horizon - all you see
from here are two vertical lines.

121 KM; 248.6 Miles (248.6S / 4.4N)
White sand dunes on right.

123 KM; 249.9 Miles (249.9S / 3.1N)
Road right.

125 KM; 251.1 Miles (251.1S / 1.9N)
Airport road to right.

127 KM; 252.3Miles (252.3S / 0.7N; el. 30 ft.)
Monumento Aguila.   This 140 feet high steel monument,
an artist's rendition of an eagle, commemorates the completion
of the Transpeninsular Highway.   It also marks the 28th
parallel, separating the states of Baja California and Baja
California Sur. It further marks the boundary of Pacific and
Mountain Standard time - move your watch ahead 1 hour. La
Pinta Hotel and RV park are nearby - both open, though there
is no electricity at the park. If you look to the left toward the
Pemex (abandoned) side of the divided road, you will see a
huge osprey nest atop the signpost.

128 KM; 253.0 Miles (253.0S / 0.0 N; el. 10 ft.)
Guerrero Negro is 2.5 kilometers to the right from the
junction.

Stylized eagle monument at Guerrero Negro marks the 28th parallel, which divides the states of Baja California and Baja California Sur

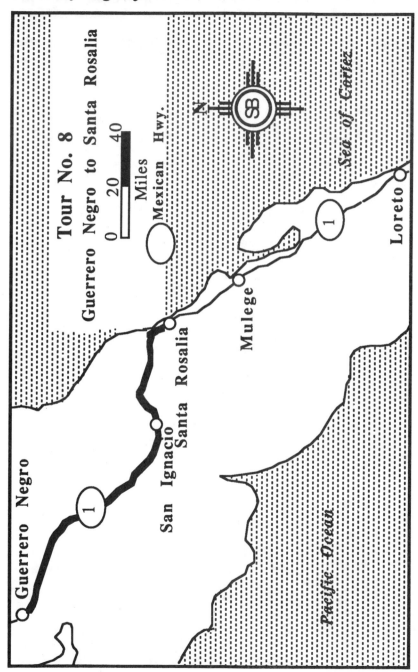

Tour No. 8
Guerrero Negro to Santa Rosalia

TOUR NO. 8 - GUERRERO NEGRO TO SANTA ROSALIA

Length: 217 KM / 135 Miles

Time Required: Two to three days

Season: October to April

Difficulty: Average

Leaving Guerrero Negro the road continues its crossing of the great Vizcaino Desert (3" annual rainfall) on a flat and straight as an arrow road. The landscape is featureless until the Ejido Vizcaino Junction is reached and cacti reappear. The last twenty miles into San Ignacio find a few rolling hills and several volcanic cones come into view. Continuing south from San Ignacio and more rolling hills, the road skirts the base of Las Tres Virgenes, three volcanic multi-colored cones which dominate the landscape. After a cactus-covered plateau is crossed, the road offers a sweeping view of the Sea of Cortez and then drops sharply to meet it at the shores of Santa Rosalia. Welcome to the Cortez side!

General:

Now you're in the State of Baja California Sur and the only noticeable difference is that the kilometers shown on the posts get smaller, instead of larger, going south. The desert area already encountered continues to San Ignacio. The first sight of San Ignacio is perhaps the epitome of the desert traveler's image of a desert palm oasis. It has certainly been an impressionable sight to many a hot and weary cyclist. After San Ignacio the desert continues through rolling hills and areas indicative of volcanic activity, on to Santa Rosalia and the Sea of Cortez.

Point of Entry: Guerrero Negro

Guerrero Negro's contribution to Baja is also to Mexico itself. Guerrero Negro is one of the leading salt producers of the world. The economic base of this company town (pop. 5,000) lies in the salt beds stretching from town south to the shores of Scammons Lagoon. Guerrero Negro (black warrior) was never of much interest to me until the winter of 1986 when I took an excellent whale watching tour (see "Excursions Within Baja," Appendix). As you enter town and ride through it, a good dirt road leads out about five miles to Puerto Venustiano. Of interest here is the salt water marsh area that is host to many different birds. The road is elevated a few feet above the marsh and affords some excellent views. At the end of the road you may be lucky enough to see some whales in season from the old dock area. This is where the whale trip, which I mentioned, originates.

Logistics:

Good bus service exists between the major cities of Baja and Guerrero Negro as well as Santa Rosalia. Ferry service to and from mainland Mexico is available at Santa Rosalia. Services in both Guerrero Negro and Santa Rosalia are quite varied and good. As you enter Guerrero Negro, Malarrimo Restaurant and the trailer park on the right cater to tourists. The Dunas and El Morro Motels are side by side, clean and inexpensive. Also found are several cafes (good inexpensive fish dinners at Veracruz and Lupita), fruit stands, supermarkets, three *panaderias, tortillerias*, a marginal motel by the bus station, a bank and hospital.

Route Log

The kilometer readings shown refer to those shown on kilometer posts along the route.

217 KM; 0.0 Miles (0.0S / 134.5N)
Leave **Guerrero Negro.**

211 KM; 3.7 Miles (3.7S / 130.8N)
Road right.

208 KM; 5.6 Miles (5.6S / 128.9N)
Turn off to the right for **Ojo de Liebre,** more commonly known as **Scammons Lagoon.** It is 15 miles on a good dirt road to the lagoon.

206 KM; 6.8 Miles (6.8S / 127.7N)
Roads right.

199 KM; 11.2 Miles (11.2S / 123.3N)
Roads right.

196 KM; 13.0 Miles (13.0S / 121.5N)
Roads right.

195 KM; 13.6 Miles (13.6S / 120.9N)
Road left to **Ejido Benito Juarez.**

190 KM; 16.7 Miles (16.7S / 117.8N)
Road left to **El Arco**. **Microondas Parrallelo El Arco** is
the first of 23 microwave stations for telephone service in Baja
California Sur. Generally situated atop promontories, you
know you're topping a hill when these stations are located
close to the roadside. Some are quite a distance away from the
road.

162 KM; 34.1 Miles (34.1S / 100.4N)
Road left.

159 KM; 36.0 Miles (36.0 S / 98.5N)
Cultivation starts.

149 KM; 42.2 Miles (42.2S / 92.3N)
Road right.

148 KM; 42.8 Miles (42.8S / 91.7N)
Road left.

144 KM; 45.3 Miles (45.3S / 89.2N; el. 260 ft.)
Ejido Vizcaino junction - the town of **Vizcaino** is 0.8 miles
to the right on a paved road. On the highway are three
loncherias, an *abarrotes*, abandoned trailer park, Pemex,
and a modest motel on the left, behind Restaurant La Huerta.
This junction is definitely growing. The road west goes to
Bahia Tortugus on the coast of the Vizcaino Peninsula.

139 KM; 48.4 Miles (48.4S / 86.1N)
Road left.

138 KM; 49.0 Miles (49.0 S / 85.5N)
Road left.

133 KM; 52.1 Miles (52.1S / 82.4N)
Road right to **Ramal Emiliano Zapata.**

125 KM; 57.0 Miles (57.0S / 77.5N)
Microondas Los Angeles.

118 KM; 61.4 Miles (61.4 S / 73.1N)
Road left to **Ramal Francisco de la Sierra**, 37 KM.

113 KM; 64.5 Miles (64.5S / 70.0N)
Roads right.

107 KM; 68.2 Miles (68.2S / 66.3N)
Roads right.

98 KM; 73.8 Miles (73.8S / 60.7N)
Road right to **Punta Abreojos** - pop stop.

89 KM; 79.4 Miles (79.4S / 55,1N)
Microondas Abulon.

77 KM; 86.8 Miles (86.8S / 47.7N)
Restaurant Quiche on right - agricultural inspection station on left.

74 KM; 88.7 Miles (88.7S / 45.8N; el. 410 ft.)
Road right to **San Lino** and **Paredones**, two small "suburbs" of **San Ignacio.** Trailer park behind the Pemex and *conosupo*. **San Ignacio** - population 2,000. The 2 KM date palm lined road into town is alien after some 500 miles of desert. Dates are the chief crop here, along with citrus and grapes. Their existence goes back to the Jesuits, who founded a mission here in 1728 and planted the date trees. The church is very well preserved, thanks to the four-foot thick walls, and is still active today. This large stone mission faces a plaza beautifully shaded by huge laurel trees. The plaza, of course, is lined by local businesses. Happily, San Ignacio has been little changed by tourists. People stop to peek into the church,

take a couple of photos, buy a bag of dates and then leave. If this lovely town were on the coast it would be a different story all together. The town has long served as a commercial center for the many fish camps on Laguna San Ignacio and for the large, but scattered, goat and cattle ranches. A tour to the mysterious cave paintings can be taken here (see "Excursions," Appendix). Being isolated, very tranquil and having a Mexican flavor all its own, San Ignacio is well worth a stop-over. At the highway there are campsites among the date palms. These are located both before and after La Pinta Hotel (signs designate both camp areas). On the Plaza is Loncheria Chalita with good, reasonably priced meals. There are also three different grocery markets, a fruit and vegetable shop, a bank and telephone service. Another cafe and *paleteria* is just beyond the *correo*. Beyond the school is La Posada Motel - less luxurious and expensive than La Pinta.

73 KM; 89.3 Miles (89.3S / 45.2N)
Seafood Restaurant (Mariscos).

71 KM; 90.5 Miles (90.5S / 44.0 N)
Tire repair and cafe.

69 KM; 91.8 Miles (91.9 S / 42.7N)
Uphill.

67 KM; 93.0 Miles (93.0 S / 41.5N)
Summit.

63 KM; 95.5 Miles (95.5S / 39.0 N)
Nice stand of yuccas begins.

60 KM; 97.3 Miles (97.3S / 37.2N)
Dirt road left for **Rancho Santa Marta.**

53 KM; 101.7 Miles (101.7S / 32.8N)
Ejido Alfredo *Loncheria.*

35 KM; 112.8 Miles (112.8S / 21.7N)
Microondas Almeja.

18 KM; 123.4 Miles (123.4S / 11.1N)
First view of **Sea of Cortez** - start very steep, curvy, downhill use **CAUTION**. Microondas.

13 KM; 126.5 Miles (126.5S / 8.0 N; el. 360 ft.)
Summit.

8 KM; 129.6 Miles (129.6S / 4.9N; el. 10 ft.)
Reach shoreline and follow into town.

0.0 KM; 134.5 Miles (134.5S / 0.0 N)
Enter **Santa Rosalia.**

Colin Warner camping in yucca grove

Bell tower of Mission Santa Rosalia in Mulege

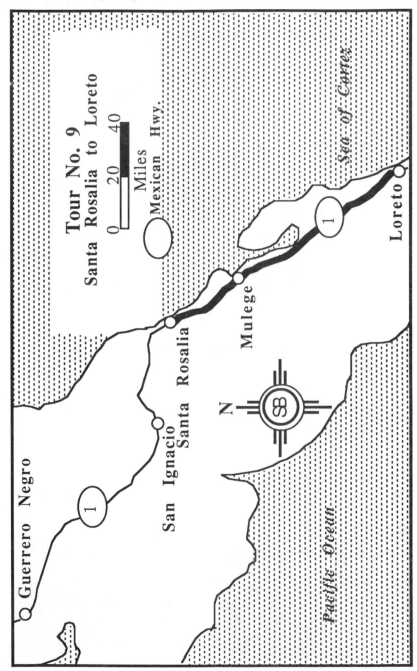

Tour No. 9
Santa Rosalia to Loreto

TOUR NO. 9 - SANTA ROSALIA TO LORETO

Length: 196 KM / 122 Miles

Time Required: Two to three days

Season: October to April

Difficulty: Average

The road follows the coast, leaving Santa Rosalia only a short distance back before climbing a hill inland. The sea stays in view with easy access near San Lucas. After San Bruno sight of the water disappears. The road crosses rolling hills with beautifully vegetated areas and sharp, mountainous peaks as the backdrop. One sharp climb occurs just before coasting into Mulege. After the road crosses the bridge over the Rio Santa Rosalia (the only navigable river in Baja) coastal views reappear as do the rolling hills, but with little vegetation. A summit is finally reached, revealing a dramatic view of the northern end of Bahia de la Concepcion. I have some photos of this beach when it is was an empty place and we joyously explored it without interruption. Those days are gone, as your view now wanders down Santispac beach, lined with its RV's and campers and with the water dotted with colorful boats of all types. For nearly 25 miles the road rolls in and out along this beautiful bay before making a substantial climb away from the coast. Topping this hill the road proceeds along an open plain. Here sunsets and sunrises provide breath-taking panoramas of the Sierra de la Giganta silhouetted against the sky. There are at least two ranchos where food may be obtained, as the road passes through more rolling hills. After these hills, with their scrub vegetation, the road makes a pleasant descent to the junction of the road into Loreto. The Loreto road is seen long before it is reached.

General:

This section includes the most tourist oriented area of the southern peninsula, with the exception of the cape region.

Likewise, it's a favorite with cyclists, with more beach access than previously encountered.

Point of Entry: Santa Rosalia
Santa Rosalia has a population of 14,000. Your first impression of this city, made just before entering, is that you are nearing an American, company-owned mining town, rather than a Mexican city. Its mining operations have slowed, but its colorful history dates back to the 1880s when rich copper deposits were discovered. Riding along Avenida Revolucion into town, the wood frame buildings, balconies and wooden sidewalks look like something out of a U.S. western movie - until you get to the church. The church doesn't look Mexican nor like anything out of the old west. The story goes that it was designed by A. G. Eiffel (of Eiffel tower fame) for the 1898 Paris World's Fair. The prefabricated structure of galvanized iron sheets was shipped in sections around Cape Horn to Santa Rosalia in Baja California. Some say it was meant for a French city having a similar name. Whatever, it has some fine stained glass windows over the altar and is rightfully the landmark of the town.

Logistics:
Avenida Revolucion is the one-way street into town   and Avenida Constitucion is the one-way out. Between these two streets you will find most of the services you may be looking for. There are several cafes, markets, a *paleteria,* fruit stand, bank, garage, and a very popular bakery (opens 11 a.m. and 3 p.m. and sells hot rolls called *bollos*). There is a hospital and the old French Hotel to the right at the church, up on the plateau. There is also telephone service and bus service to the major cities of Baja. The modern ferry terminal at the small harbor provides service across the **Sea of Cortez** to **Guaymas** (see Part 2, "Logistics; Public Transportation").

Services in **Mulege** include: Hotels Rosita, Casitas, Hacienda and the modern Vista Hermosa; there are several cafes and restaurants, a supermarket with lots of American products, fruit stands, *tortilleria,* laundromat, bank, telephone, garage and small gift shops. Camping and other hotels are located south of the bridge.

Route Log:

The kilometer readings shown refer to those shown on kilometer posts along the route.

196 KM; 0.0 Miles (0.0S / 121.5N; el. 10 ft.)
Leave Santa Rosalia. Road passes Microondas Santa Rosalia.

195 KM; 0.6 Miles (0.6S / 120.9N)
Hotel El Morro - on the water.

193 KM; 1.9 Miles (1.9S / 119.6N; el. 80 ft.)
Uphill.

190 KM; 3.7 Miles (3.7S / 117.8N; el. 340 ft.)
Summit.

189 KM; 4.3 Miles (4.3S / 117.2N)
New prison replacing the old one in Mulege.

188 KM; 5.0 Miles (5.0S / 116.5N)
Road right to **Ramal Agueda.**

185 KM; 6.8 Miles (6.8S / 114.7N)
Roads right and left.

182 KM; 8.7 Miles (8.7S / 112.8N; el. 40 ft.)
Road to **San Lucas RV park** and camping.

180 KM; 9.9 Miles (9.9S / 111.6N)
Road to public beach. Road right for **Microondas San Lucas.**

172 KM; 14.9 Miles (14.9S / 106.6N; el. 60 ft.)
Cafe and sodas. Rest of **San Bruno** to the left on the beach.

169 KM; 16.7 Miles (16.7S / 104.8N)
Ramal to right.

167 KM; 18.0 Miles (18.0S / 103.5N)
Microondas S.J. de Magdelena.

162 KM; 21.1 Miles (21.1S / 100.4N).
Road left to SCT *campimento.*

156 KM; 24.8 Miles (24.8S / 96.7N)
Ejido San Lucas - pop stop on left.

144 KM; 32.2 Miles (32.2S / 89.3N)
Airport road to right (no commercial flights).

142 KM; 33.5 Miles (33.5S / 88.0 N; el. 160 ft.)
Uphill.

139 KM; 35.3 Miles (35.3S / 86.2N; el. 400 ft.)
Summit.

136 KM; 37.2 Miles (37.2S / 84.3N; el. 20 ft.)
Mulege - population 6,000. Mulege is the second date palm, oasis-like town in this series of tours (the first was San Ignacio) and is obviously much more to the liking of tourists. Many facilities have been built to provide services to promote tourism. The town itself is located primarily on the north shore of the **Rio Santa Rosalia**, a little over a mile upstream from where the river flows into the sea. The lush vegetation, mostly date palms, is again the result of the Jesuits who founded the Mission Santa Rosalia de Mulege in 1705. The large mission is easily sighted among the palms while coming down the hill into town. To get to the mission, cross the bridge and turn left as if going to the campground (seen from the highway). Go back under the bridge and keep the river on your right. The mission is approximately 0.5 miles from the bridge. Seen from the bridge, or in town, the dominant, large white building was formerly the Federal Territorial Prison. The prison has been relocated south of Santa Rosalia and is now a museum.

135 KM; 37.8 Miles (37.8S / 83.7N)
Bridge crossing **Rio Santa Rosalia.**

134 KM; 38.4 Miles (38.4S / 83.1N)
RV parks - Jorges, Rancho Orchard.

133 KM; 39.1 Miles (39.1S / 82.4N)
Villas Maria Isabella RV park - terrific bakery.

132 KM; 39.7 Miles (39.7S / 81.8N)
Turn off for Hotel Serenidad.

131 KM; 40.3 Miles (40.3S / 81.2N)
El Tiburon Restaurant - also at the top of 1 KM hill.

124 KM; 44.6 Miles (44.6S / 76.9N)
Microondas Tiburones.

119 KM; 47.7 Miles (47.7S / 73.8N)
Road left to **Punta Arena** - some distance to the beach.

114 KM; 50.8 Miles (50.8S / 70.7N; el. 310 ft.)
Top of hill.

113 KM; 51.5 Miles (51.5S / 70.0N; el. 0 ft.)
Playa de Santispac - first camping beach on **Bahia Concepcion.** Also Anna's bakery and cafe.

112 KM; 52.1 Miles (52.1S / 69.4N)
Posada Concepcion - *tienda* of limited supplies across from trailer park.

111 KM 52.7 Miles (52.7S / 68.8N)
Los Cocos - beach access.

110 KM; 53.3 Miles (53.3S / 68.2N)
Beach access - there is a cluster of pictographs on rocks on the right side of the road, just before the left turn for the beach. There is a small turnout on the left side of the road. Rancho El Coyote - Estrella del Mar restaurant - on right.

109 KM; 53.9 Miles (53.9S / 67.6N)
El Coyote - beach access. Go through the archway making a hard right to the public beach. There's a fresh water spring at the beach.

108 KM; 54.6 Miles (54.6S / 66.9N)
Beach access.

104 KM; 57.0 Miles (57.0S / 64.5N; el. 300 ft.)
Top of climb after El Coyote.

101 KM; 58.9 Miles (58.9S / 62.6N)
Road right.

96 KM; 62.0 Miles (62.0S / 59.5N)
Beach access.

95 KM; 62.6 Miles (62.6S / 58.9N)
Beach access with defunct rancho.

93 KM; 63.9 Miles (63.9S / 57.6N)
Playa El Requeson - last good sandy beach. At low-tide a sand spit connects the small island to the crescent shaped beach.

91 KM; 65.1 Miles (65.1S / 56.4N)
Playa Armenta.

88 KM; 67.0 Miles (67.0S / 54.5N)
Beach access - not signed.

85 KM; 68.8 Miles (68.8S / 52.7N)
Beach access.

78 KM; 73.2 Miles (73.2S / 48.3N)
Rancho - pop stop.

76 KM; 74.4 Miles (74.4S / 47.1N)
Abandoned trailer park on left - this dirt road will go on around Concepcion.

75 KM; 75.0 Miles (75.0S / 46.5N)
Uphill.

68 KM; 79.4 Miles (79.4S / 42.1N)
Summit. Microondas Rosarito.

66 KM; 80.6 Miles (80.6S / 40.9N)
Road right.

63 KM; 82.5 Miles (82.5S / 39.0N)
Rancho Rosarito - sometimes a pop stop.

53 KM; 88.7 Miles (88.7S / 32.8N; el. 340 ft.)
Rancho Bombedor - good meals and water.

23 KM; 107.3 Miles (107.3S / 14.2N)
Rancho - pop stop.

18 KM; 110.4 Miles (110.4S / 11.1N)
Uphill.

15 KM; 112.2 Miles (112.2S / 9.3N)
Summit.

9 KM; 115.9 Miles (115.9S / 5.6N)
Microondas Loreto.

7 KM; 117.2 Miles (117.2S / 4.3N; el. 300 ft.)
Top of hill - **Loreto** in view.

6 KM; 117.8 Miles (117.8S / 3.7N)
Rancho Miramar - *loncheria.*

3 KM; 119.7 Miles (119.7S / 1.8N)
Edge of town.

0 KM; 121.5 Miles (121.5S / 0.0N)
Left turn into **Loreto.**

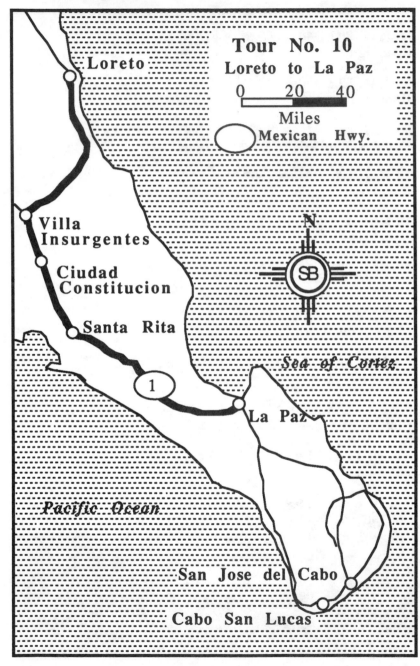

Tour No. 10
Loreto to La Paz

TOUR NO. 10- LORETO TO LA PAZ

Length: 357 KM; 221 Miles

Time Required: Five to seven days

Season: October to April

Difficulty: Difficult

This route takes in a coastal roller coaster, the second major hill climb of Highway 1, and the start of the hot, dry, flat and sparsely vegetated **Magdelena Plain.** Be sure your water bottles are full. After reaching the flats of **Villa Insurgentes,** the next 15 miles require the cyclist to ride with **CAUTION.** This bit of roadway, between two very busy farming cities, has as much traffic as in La Paz and on the stretch between the two Cabos. Beyond **Ciudad Constitucion** is a very flat, barren and boring 30 miles to Santa Rita. Often there is a cool fog in the morning that quickly burns off. From **Santa Rita** the gentle, rolling hills resume, getting steeper after Rancho San Agustin. When the hills culminate, with a grand view of La Paz Bay, it is a rolling down-hill to the coastline. The road then follows the curving bay into the city of **La Paz.**

General:

Situated on the beach side of a coastal plain with dramatic and rugged mountains as a backdrop, **Loreto** is a natural area for tourist development. The main tourist attraction? Sport fishing. Loreto has been a popular fly-in fishing spot for years, yet, with a recent upgrading of paved roads in town and several new modern hotel accommodations, they hope to spread the growth of the tourist trade. A big step in that direction was the re-opening of the Loreto airport with a paved jet runway in the early 1980s. The **Loreto-Puerto Escondido** area is the next Baja Fonatur (government managed development group) complex. Even with such changes there still remain quiet beaches for the cycle tourist to find and explore.

The route passes over the **Magdalena Plain**, formerly a broad, arid region, now one of the major agricultural regions of Baja. The transformation was brought about by the drilling of deep, water wells throughout the area. The arid area resumes after leaving Ciudad Constitucion, developing into hills as the coast is approached.

Point of Entry: Loreto

Loreto - population 8,000. Loreto is the site of the first permanent settlement of the Baja peninsula dating back to 1697 when the Jesuit Juan Maria Salvatierra arrived and founded the "Mother Mission" - Mission Nuestra Senora de Loreto. A visit to the museum adjacent to the mission is worthwhile. The town prospered and remained the capital of Baja until 1829, when a hurricane destroyed the community and the capital was moved to La Paz.

Logistics:

Camping facilities in or close to Loreto have come and gone in years past with one presently open. The beaches south of Loreto offer camping on a primitive and deluxe basis. Other major development includes a luxury El Presidente Hotel at Nopolo and the Tripui trailer park on the Puerto Escondido road. This is like no other on the peninsula, complete with clean swimming pool and immaculate maintenance. Limited, but ample services may be found in both Loreto and Villa Insurgentes.

Route Log

The kilometer readings shown refer to those shown on kilometer posts along the route.

120 KM; 0.0 Miles (0.0S / 221.3; el. 40 ft.)
Leave **Loreto** at Highway 1 turning south.

118 KM; 1.2 Miles (1.2S / 220.1N)
Road right to **San Javier** (See Rough Stuff - Mountain Bike Tours)

117 KM; 1.9 Miles (1.9S / 219.4N)
Paved road left to airport.

112 KM; 5.0 Miles (5.0S / 216.3N)
El Presidente Hotel, site of resort complex. Road also goes to **Nopolo** beach.

108 KM; 7.4 Miles (7.4S / 213.9N).
Dirt road left to **Notri** - no sign - watch the tide here.

104 KM; 9.9 Miles (9.9S / 211.4N)
Road right.

103 KM; 10.5 Miles (10.5S / 210.8N)
Beach access - rocky, close road.

98 KM; 13.6 Miles (13.6S / 207.7N)
Playa Juncalito - be careful on road in; trees on right side drop thorns into the road.

95 KM; 15.5 Miles (15.5S / 205.8N)
Paved road left to **Puerto Escondido** - hotel complex being built. Halfway to the beach is the well kept Tripui trailer park which has tents with bunk beds for campers (no tenting area). An expensive restaurant is also at the park.

86 KM; 21.1 Miles (21.1S / 200.2N)
Road left.

85 KM; 21.7 Miles (21.7S / 199.6N; el. 40 ft.)
Rancho Ligui. There is a gate in the fence providing public access to the beach beyond. Distance is about 1 mile. At the Y, stay left.

83 KM; 22.9 Miles (22.9S / 198.4N; el. 60 ft.)
Giant hill starts - fairly steep at first, it makes a big U-curve, then a switchback and continues the climb.

79 KM; 25.4 Miles (25.4S / 195.9N; 840 ft.)
Top of the steep climb, but road is still climbing.

77 KM; 26.7 Miles (26.7S / 194.6N; 1100 ft.)
Most of the climbing over with, although road still has a gentle grade.

71 KM; 30.4 Miles (30.4S / 190.9N; 1140 ft.)
Microondas Ligui - good shade tree on left.

64 KM; 34.7 Miles (34.7S / 186.9 N)
Road to **Agua Verde** to left.

61 KM; 36.6 Miles (36.6S / 184.7N)
Road left to large clearing with shade, camping sites.

55 KM; 40.3 Miles (40.3S / 181.0N)
Rancho on left - no services.

51 KM; 42.8 Miles (42.8S / 178.5N)
Rancho on left - no services.

46 KM; 45.9 Miles (45.9S / 175.4N; el. 1180 ft.)
Microondas Agua Amarga - top of all hills.

44 KM; 47.1 Miles (47.1S / 174.2N)
Road left. From KM 46 it is a gradual, downhill run to Villa
Insurgentes. Heading west, there is invariably a headwind
here in the afternoon. If camping here, pick a side road before
KM 34. It can be quite foggy and damp in the morning the
closer you are to town and the irrigated fields. Staying higher,
stays drier.

43 KM; 47.7 Miles (47.7S / 173.6N)
Road right.

40 KM; 49.6 Miles (49.6S / 171.7N)
Road right.

33 KM; 53.9 Miles (53.9S / 167.4N)
Road right.

31 KM; 55.2 Miles (55.2S / 166.1N)
Road right.

30 KM; 55.8 Miles (55.8S / 165.5N)
Road left.

22 KM; 60.8 Miles (60.8S / 160.5N)
Road left.

17 KM; 63.9 Miles (63.9S / 157.4N)
Pemex with sodas, cafe next door. This marks the end of cactus and cultivated fields; then, traffic and people begin.

0 KM; 74.4 Miles (74.4S / 146.9N)
Villa Insurgentes, population 8,000.   This agricultural center has boomed along with **Ciudad Constitucion.** Being the smaller of the two cities, Villa Insurgentes always seems a little dirtier, rougher and less friendly to outsiders. Maybe I have never spent enough time here to get to know the place, as I prefer Constitucion, a growing favorite with cyclists.

Highway 1 with Rene Freret on the last, long, downhill run into La Paz

237 KM; 74.4 Miles (74.4S / 146.9 N)
Leaving Villa Insurgentes. Note the change in kilometer
post numbering from Villa Insugentes south.

236 KM; 75.0 Miles (75.0 S / 146.3N)
Sign for La Paz, some small stores and several pop stops.

228 KM; 80.0 Miles (80.0 S / 141.3N)
Pop stop.

224 KM; 82.5 Miles (82.5S / 138.8N)
Road right.

211 KM; 90.5 Miles (90.5 S / 130.1N)
Pop stop.

210 KM; 91.1 Miles (91.1S / 130.2N)
Ciudad Constitucion - population 44,000.   Ciudad
Constitucion is the agricultural center of lower Baja. When I
first saw this town in 1973 it looked much like what San
Quintin looks like today. However, the town has grown and
expresses a confident air of prosperity and well being. The
reasons for the change are the deep wells drilled into the
underlying "fossil water" lakes, which provide the irrigation
water necessary for crops. Cotton is king here. It is exported
from the deep water port at San Carlos, some 35 miles
distant, on the Pacific.

Highway 1 becomes divided here with parallel frontage roads
lending access to the many businesses lining the main
thoroughfare.   Four stop lights emphasize the fact that you
are truly in a city. Ciudad Constitucion is busy, people are
well dressed, the buildings are well maintained, and there are
refreshing tree shaded plazas throughout.

Though not a tourist destination at all, Ciudad Constitucion is
becoming a favorite with cyclists. What could be of interest to
cyclists? Food, of course. Whether eating out or stocking up
for a night at the local campground, a visit to the public
marketplace is a must. The numerous stalls are housed in a
covered building, taking up an entire block. Row upon row of

meat, fish, vegetables, exotic fruit, *tortilleria, paleteria,* fresh squeezed fruit juices, and *liquados* vie for your attention. There are several stalls of dry goods also. Turn left on Olachea Hidalgo (the stop light after the Pemex). It is then one block to the marketplace. Other services include: several hotels, supermarkets with U.S. products, restaurants, hospital, bank, telephone, laundromat, bike shop, and a campground on the south end of town. Restaurant Las Brisas, also at the south end of town, has good seafood dinners.

198 KM; 98.6 Miles (98.6S / 122.7N)
Loncheria, abarrotes.

180 KM; 109.7 Miles (109.7S / 111.6N)
Road left.

178 KM; 111.0 Miles (111.0S / 110.3N)
Road left.

174 KM; 113.5 Miles (113.5S / 107.8 N)
Road right to **Cancun,** 32 KM.

169 KM; 116.6Miles (116.6S / 104.7N)
Microondas Torete.

164 KM; 119.7 Miles (119.7S / 101.6N)
Road right.

157 KM; 124.0 Miles (124.0 S / 97.3N; el. 100 ft.)
Santa Rita - essentially a wide spot in the road. Most of this small community is off to the left. Los Pinos restaurant (rancho style), on the left, has reasonable meals and drinks. Another place, on the right side of the road, has sodas, beer and limited groceries.

155 KM; 50.8 Miles (50.8S / 96.1N)
Loncheria on right.

152 KM; 52.7 Miles (52.7S / 94.2N)
Road right.

148 KM; 129.6 Miles (129.6S / 91.7N)
Roads right and left.

141 KM; 133.9 Miles (133.9S / 87.4N)
Road right.

140 KM; 134.5 Miles (134.5S / 86.8N)
Road right - camping good.

135 KM; 137.6 Miles (137.6S / 83.7N)
Microondas El Rifle.

130 KM; 140.7 Miles (140.7S / 80.6N)
Road right - good camping spot.

128 KM; 142.0 Miles (142.0 S / 79.3N)
Rancho Rosita - meals and drinks. Roads right and left.

Casey Patterson riding south of Puerto Escondido on Highway 1. Sierra de la Giganta in background

124 KM; 144.5 Miles (144.5S / 76.8N)
Roads right and left.

118 KM; 148.2 Miles (148.2S / 73.1N)
Loncheria. Road right to **Ramal Santa Fe**, 16 KM.

114 KM; 150.7 Miles (150.7S / 70.6N)
Loncheria Rosy.

113 KM; 151.3 Miles (151.3S / 70.0N; el. 480 ft.)
Las Pocitas - *loncheria*, mission, Red Cross, a growing *ejido*.

111 KM; 152.5 Miles (152.5S / 68.8N)
Benjamo Cafe on left.

102 KM; 158.1 Miles (158.1S / 63.2N)
Road left.

100 KM; 159.3 Miles (159.3S / 62.0N; el. 500 ft.)
El Cien - cafe with sodas and sandwiches next to Pemex.

98 KM; 160.6 Miles (160.6S / 60.7N)
Road left.

96 KM; 161.8 Miles (161.8S / 59.5N)
Tere Cafe. Road left to **Guadalupe del Herradero.**

90 KM; 165.5 Miles (165.5S / 55.8N)
Road right.

88 KM; 166.8 Miles (166.8S / 54.5N)
Road right.

86 KM; 168.0 Miles (168.0 S / 53.3N)
Road left.

82 KM; 170.5 Miles (170.5S / 50.8N)
Microondas El Coyote.

81 KM; 171.1 Miles (171.1S / 50.2N)
Road right to **Conejo**, 17 KM.

77 KM; 173.6 Miles (173.6S / 47.7N)
Road left.

76 KM; 174.2 Miles (174.2S / 47.1N; el. 340 ft.)
Restaurant San Agustin - good meals.

75 KM; 174.8 Miles (174.8S / 46.5N)
Uphill.

74 KM; 175.5 Miles (175.5S / 45.8N)
Summit.

71 KM; 177.3 Miles (177.3S / 44.0 N)
Road right.

Troy Bott, Mary Ann Bott, Wolfgang Hauser at typical "pop stop," Santa Rita

70 KM; 177.9 Miles (177.9S / 43.4N)
Uphill.

68 KM; 179.2 Miles (179.2S / 42.1N; el. 800 ft.)
Summit.

62 KM; 182.9 Miles (182.9S / 38.4N; el. 1000 ft.)
White plaster cardon cactus.

61 KM; 183.5 Miles (183.5S / 37.8N)
Faint road right.

60 KM; 184.1 Miles (184.1S / 37.2N)
Microondas El Cardon.

56 KM; 186.6 Miles (186.6S / 34.7N)
Old road right. A short distance beyond is a newer road right (it has power poles). Proceed 0.6 miles along this newer road to a side road at the right. This is an excellent campsite.

47 KM; 192.2 Miles (192.2 Miles / 29.1N; el. 900 ft.)
Road right.

45 KM; 193.4 Miles (193.4S / 27.9N)
Restaurant on right.

38 KM; 197.8 Miles (197.8S / 23.5N)
Road right to **Referma Agara.**

36 KM; 199.0 Miles (199.0 S / 22.3N)
Microondas Matape. Road right.

35 KM; 199.6 Miles (199.6S / 21.7N)
Shrine on right - top of hill with long rolling downhill.

28 KM; 204.0 Miles (204.0 S / 17.3N)
Rancho 28 - no services - ends downhill.

27 KM; 204.6 Miles (204.6S / 16.7N)
Road left to **Ramal Alfredo Bonfil.**

20 KM; 208.9 Miles (208.9S / 12.4N)
Road right - fences start.

17 KM; 210.8 Miles (210.8S / 10.5N; el. 80 ft.)
Paved road left to **San Juan de la Costa.**

15 KM; 212.0 Miles (212.0 S / 9.3N)
Oasis Los Aripez trailer park.   English spoken on the
beach; hot showers, bar.

10 KM; 215.1 Miles (215.1S / 6.2N)
El Centenario - small community with pop stop, *tortilleria.*

8 KM; 216.4 Miles (216.4S / 4.9N)
Paved road right to airport.   **Restaurant Rodeo** at this
junction, sometimes it is operating.

6 KM; 217.6 Miles (217.6S / 3.7N)
Left at Y for "**El Centro**" or right on **Graza** turnoff for
Cabo San Lucas.

4 KM; 218.9 Miles (218.9S / 2.4N)
El Cardon trailer park on right - has hot showers, swimming
pool, laundromat and shaded sites.   Another trailer park to the
left, which is closer to the beach but has only cement slabs and
no shade - is not for tenting.

2 KM; 220.1 Miles (220.1S / 1.2N)
Pemex on left and good *panaderia* on right corner.   This street
is 5 de Febrero.   Take a right turn here for **Cabo San Lucas**
- or left, when coming from La Paz city center.

0 KM; 221.3 Miles (221.3S / 0.0 N)
La Paz.

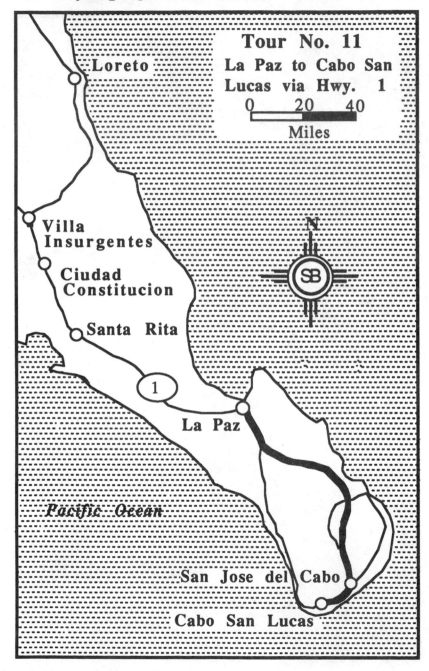

Tour No. 11
La Paz to Cabo San Lucas via Hwy. 1

0   20   40
Miles

TOUR NO. 11- LA PAZ TO CABO SAN LUCAS VIA HIGHWAY 1

Length: 221 KM / 137 Miles

Time Required: Two to three days

Season: October to April

Difficulty: Average

From La Paz there is a long, gradual climb to San Pedro which slowly gets steeper as El Triunfo is approached. A steep climb is made after El Triunfo, a sharp descent to San Antonio followed by another steep grade. Rolling hills are encountered, with the road tending upward until San Bartolo is reached. From that canyon town it is mostly downhill to the Sea of Cortez at Buena Vista. Heading inland again, the road climbs through rolling hills then starts a long, gradual downhill to San Jose del Cabo. The last 20 miles to Cabo San Lucas is a roller coaster reminiscent of the many hilly miles previously traveled.

General:

The route via Highway 1 to Cabo San Lucas is hilly, dry and passes through several small towns. It touches the Sea of Cortez at Bahia de Palmas and parallels the seashore for about 20 miles from San Jose del Cabo to Cabo San Lucas

Point of Entry: La Paz

La Paz - population 110,000. La Paz or "the peace" became so in spite of a slow and turbulent start. The Spaniards stopped here as early as 1533 but hostile Indians prevented settlement. Supply problems prevented other attempts from success. Not until 1811 did settlement endure and then the capital was moved from Loreto to La Paz in 1829. Pearling was the main industry until the1940s. Today, La Paz is a modern city, attractively located beside the bay where travelers

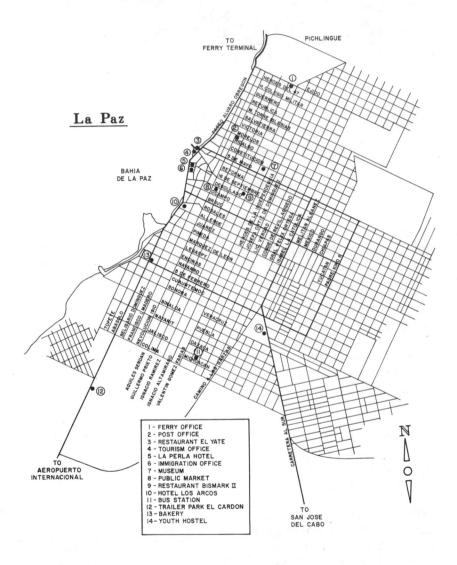

La Paz

1 - FERRY OFFICE
2 - POST OFFICE
3 - RESTAURANT EL YATE
4 - TOURISM OFFICE
5 - LA PERLA HOTEL
6 - IMMIGRATION OFFICE
7 - MUSEUM
8 - PUBLIC MARKET
9 - RESTAURANT BISMARK II
10 - HOTEL LOS ARCOS
11 - BUS STATION
12 - TRAILER PARK EL CARDON
13 - BAKERY
14 - YOUTH HOSTEL

can take a ferry to mainland Mexico. If La Paz is the destination itself, this resort city has a lot to offer in subtle Mexican fashion without all the glitter of Cabo.

I used to resent La Paz. It was a city. There were stop lights, traffic, crowds of people and higher prices on the menu, when really the bottom line was - it was the end of the trip. La Paz meant it was time to think about returning to that "other life". I've come to accept this inevitable re-entry syndrome and now use my time in La Paz to enjoy the place! I hope you will too.

Logistics:
The services in La Paz are excellent. They include another public market place, though not as good as the one in Ciudad Constitucion, yet the bakery has good dark bread, which is unusual to find in Baja. There are two good bicycle shops. Besides bus service to the major cities of Baja, there is ferry service to Mazatlan, Topolobampo and Puerto Vallarta (see Chapter 2, Logistics, Public Transportation). The La Paz airport has international status with flights to and from many major U.S. cities. The tourist information center is located on the Tourist Wharf just past the Perla Hotel. Despite the advertised bilingual attendants, I've been in twice and no one spoke English. They do have helpful city maps, however. The Anthropology and Historical Museum of Baja is located at the corner of Ignacio Altimirano and 5 de Mayo streets. The route passes through several small towns, with nominal services, on its way to Cabo San Lucas.

Route Log:
The kilometer readings shown refer to those shown on kilometer posts along the route.

0.0 Miles (0.0S / 137.0 N)
Leaving **La Paz,** turn left at the Pemex station on Calle 5 de Febrero. Follow this road out to the wide, divided, four-lane roadway at a major intersection, sometimes signed for San Lucas. Turn right at this four-way intersection. After about 3 miles the road narrows to two lanes.

209 KM; 7.4 Miles (7.4S / 129.6N)
Motel. Road climbs very gradually, habitations thin out, fences are on both sides of the road and vegetation is sparse. Some large cardons are seen.

194 KM; 16.7 Miles (16.7S / 120.3N)
Restaurant on right has a round, thatched roof and good food.

190 KM; 19.2 Miles (19.2S / 117.8N; el. 620 ft.)
San Pedro - small village. Water is available and the El Paraiso restaurant specializes in pork *carnitas*. Plan on a meal here.

186 KM; 21.7 Miles (21.7S / 115.3N; el. 760 ft.)
Junction of Highways 1 and 19.

182 KM; 24.2 Miles (24.2S / 112.8N)
Road right to **Rancho Algones.**

178 KM; 26.7 Miles (26.7S / 110.3N).
Road right to **Ramal Divisidero.**

171 KM; 31.0 Miles (31.0S / 106.0N)
Road right.

168 KM; 32.9 Miles (32.9S / 104.1N)
Left to **Ramal El Rosario.**

166 KM; 34.1 Miles (34.1S / 102.9N; el. 1600 ft.)
Road left - top of hill.

163 KM; 36.0 Miles (36.0 S / 101.0N; el. 1500 ft.)
El Triunfo - a colorful village along the highway, nestled between hills. It is now nearly a ghost town with empty buildings. In its heyday (late 1860s) silver mining supported a sizeable population. The old smelter, inactive since the 1920s, can easily be seen from the road. More recently the village has been noted for its handwoven baskets. Available is a cafe and a very limited *conosupo.*

164 KM; 35.3 Miles (35.3S / 101.7N)
Uphill.

159 KM; 38.4 Miles (38.4S / 98.6N; el. 1880 ft.)
Summit.

156 KM; 40.3 Miles (40.3S / 96.7N; el. 1200 ft.)
San Antonio - a quiet, agricultural community located at the bottom of a steep hill. Very limited *abarrotes* and meager *loncheria*; water is available. Uphill starts immediately.

153 KM; 42.2 Miles (42.2S / 94.8N; el.1610 ft.)
Summit.

150 KM; 44.0 Miles (44.0 S / 93.0 N; el. 1160 ft.)
Roads right and left.

148 KM; 45.3 Miles (45.3S / 91.7N)
Road right to **Ramal San Antonio de la Sierra.**
Gradual downgrade becomes steeper.

147 KM; 45.9 Miles (45.9S / 91.1N)
Road left and right.

145 KM; 47.1 Miles (47.1S / 89.9N)
Road right.

139 KM; 50.8 Miles (50.8S / 86.2N)
Fences on both sides of the road.

137 KM; 52.1 Miles (52.1S / 84.9N; el. 1800 ft.)
Climbing done.

135 KM; 53.3 Miles (53.3S / 83.7N)
Road right.

130 KM; 56.4 Miles (56.4S / 80.6N)
Gradual downgrade becomes steeper.

128 KM; 57.7 Miles (57.7S / 79.3N; el. 1320 ft.)
San Bartolo - a small cluster of houses and businesses along side a palm lined canyon wall. San Bartolo is always a delight for the cyclist to come upon. Especially meaningful is the sight of the several fruit stands, well stocked with grapefruit,

oranges, avocados, papaya, various candies and fruit jellies. Besides fresh fruit, there are three good cafes, some small *abarrotes* and a pleasant plaza with drinking water. **Microondas San Bartolo** is nearby. The road continues downhill.

121 KM; 62.0 Miles (62.0 S / 75.N; el. 740 ft.)
Restaurante Pame - good meals and few supplies.

113 KM; 67.0 Miles (67.0 S / 70.0 N; el. 120 ft.)
The road goes mostly downhill to this point and crosses a wide arroyo.

111 KM; 68.2 Miles (68.2 S / 68.8N)
Restaurante Chiquis on right. Martin Verdugo Trailer Park on the beach turnoff to the left, also the turnoff for Hotel Playa Hermosa.

110 KM; 68.8 Miles (68.8S / 68.2N)
Hotel and restaurant to left.

109 KM; 69.4 Miles (69.4S / 67.6N; el. 20 ft.)
Los Barriles - Buena Vista. These two communities tend to blend together along the beach side of the road. With a landing strip and plenty of nice hotels, this is a favorite fly-in spot for fishermen. Many boats line the beach. It can often be very windy along here and windsurfing is very popular.

108 KM; 70.1 Miles (70.1S / 66.9N)
Road to beach across from Pemex. Hotel and restaurant nearby.

107 KM; 70.7 Miles (70.7S / 66.3N)
Buena Vista. Community has a restaurant, La Gaviota, the Vista del Mar Trailer Park, *abarrotes* and several houses. Road right to **Ramal Coro** - 9 KM.

106 KM; 71.3 Miles (71.3S / 65.7N)
Hotel Buena Vista.

105 KM; 71.9 Miles (71.9S / 65.1N)
Road left to Rancho Leonero and Camp Capilla on the beach.

100 KM; 75.0 Miles (75.0 S / 62.0 N)
Microondas Los Barriles.

93 KM; 79.4 Miles (79.4S / 57.6N)
Road left to **La Ribera** (see Rough Stuff (Off-Highway) Tours).

91 KM; 80.6 Miles (80.6S / 56.4N; el. 280 ft.)
Start climb.

89 KM; 81.8 Miles (81.8S / 55.2N; el. 480 ft.)
Summit. Road stays on the ridge (few camping possibilities). Rolling hills.

Ellie Winninghoff and church at El Triunfo, Highway 1

85 KM; 84.3 Miles (84.3S / 52.7N; el. 640 ft.)
Santiago is 2 KM downhill on a paved road to the right. This small community has a nice plaza with reasonably stocked *abarrotes* (2), a *farmacia* and a good cafe at the Hotel Palomar just off the plaza. The hotel is on the way to the zoo, which has a reasonable collection of Baja animals, reptiles and birds. The rancho on Highway 1 at the Santiago junction also serves meals.

82 KM; 86.2 Miles (86.2S / 50.8N)
Tropic of Cancer Monument.

74 KM; 91.1 Miles (91.1S / 45.9N; el. 800 ft.)
Microondas San Matias.

71 KM; 93.0 Miles (93.0S / 44.0 N)
Miraflores is 2 KM to the right on a paved road. If you are looking for a meal it is worth turning off here and going into town. The little restaurant at the junction greatly overprices their meals and their beer. The *cerveza deposito* tripled their beer prices when we bought there. This seems to be happening more and more, the closer you get to Los Cabos. Miraflores also has a *mercado* and is known for its leather goods, although no specific store seems to carry these items. It appears to be a home industry and you have to ask directions to find a manufacturing "home."

70 KM; 93.6 Miles (93.6S / 43.4N)
Uphill.

67 KM; 95.5 Miles (95.5S / 41.5N)
Summit.

66 KM; 96.1 Miles (96.1S / 40.9N)
Road right to **Caduano** - start uphill.

61 KM; 99.2 Miles (99.2S / 37.8N)
Microondas Caduano.

59 KM; 100.0 Miles (100.0 S / 37.0 N)
Roads right and left.

58 KM; 101.1 Miles (101.1S / 35.9N)
Uphill.

56 KM; 102.3 Miles (102.3S / 34.7N)
Summit.

55 KM; 102.9 Miles (102.9S / 34.1N)
Road right to **Ramal Naranjos.**

54 KM; 103.5 Miles (103.5S / 33.5N)
Road right.

53 KM; 104.2 Miles (104.2S / 32.8N)
Road left.

49 KM; 106.6 Miles (106.6S / 30.4N)
Road left. **Rancho Los Carroles** on right.

47 KM; 107.9 Miles (107.9S / 29.1N; el. 160 ft.)
Santa Anita.   A very small farming community.   Small
abarrotes.

45 KM; 109.1 Miles (109.1S / 27.9N)
Road right.

44 KM; 109.7 Miles (109.7S / 27.3N)
Paved road right to **Los Cabos International Airport.**
Sign: San Jose del Cabo 12 KM, Cabo San Lucas 42 KM.

41 KM: 111.6 Miles (111.6S / 25.4N)
San Bernabe - church and *cerveza.*

40 KM; 112.2 Miles (112.2S / 24.8N; el. 100 ft.)
San Jose Viejo - a growing residential community adjacent
to Cabo San Jose. *Conosupo* and a *mercado.*

38 KM; 113.5 Miles (113.5S / 23.5N)
El Zacatel - houses and school.

36 KM; 114.7 Miles (114.7S / 22.3N)
Santa Rosa - another residential community and growing
suburb of San Jose del Cabo. Cafe and *mercado.*

35 KM; 115.3 Miles (115.3S / 21.7N)

San Jose del Cabo - population 22,000. San Jose is the bigger of the two "Cabos" and has managed to retain some of its essential Mexican character and flavor. In the beach portion of town, new resorts, golf courses, and tennis courts are appearing at a rapid rate. The proximities of the airport and the ferry terminal at Cabo San Lucas have greatly opened up the area to tourists. The one-way road leading into town is lined with various businesses ending at the plaza. From there, after a sharp right turn, is the one-way road out of town. Along this street is the Chiliquinas Restaurant operated by Chilon Amora, an avid cyclist himself. Besides good food, you can get good information here. Up the same one-way road, one block on the left, is a small public marketplace. From the sharp right turn at the plaza, you can go straight to the beach and cruise by the hotel row back to Highway 1.

30 KM; 118.4 Miles (118.4S / 18.6N)

La Brisis Trailer Park on the water.

28 KM; 119.7 Miles (119.7S / 17.3N)

Small trailer park.

26 KM; 120.9 Miles (120.9S / 16.1N)

Hotel Palmilla.

25 KM; 121.5 Miles (121.5S / 15.5N)

Microondas Santa Rita.

20 KM; 124.6 Miles (124.6S / 12.4N)

Beach access. From here to Cabo San Lucas the fences along the beach side of the road have blossomed. There is space through the fence/gate for a bicycle to pass, where beaches are posted "Playas Publico" (public beach). This stretch of beach is destined for hotel and private home development. There are more rolling hills to Cabo San Lucas, and more traffic, especially after a flight has arrived at the airport.

19 KM; 125.2 Miles (125.2S / 11.8N)

Beach access with fence.

16 KM; 127.1 Miles (127.1S / 9.9N)
Beach access with fence.

14 KM; 128.3 Miles (128.3S / 8.7N)
Hotel Cabo San Lucas.

11 KM; 130.2 Miles (130.2S / 6.8N)
Hotel.

7 KM; 132.7 Miles (132.7S / 4.3N)
Microondas Santo Tomas.

6 KM; 133.3 Miles (133.3S / 3.7N)
Hotel Calinda Cabo.

5 KM; 133.9 Miles (133.9S / 3.1N)
Cafe El Arco and trailer park on right. Top of last hill.

4 KM; 134.5 Miles (134.5S / 2.5N)
Cabo Cielo trailer park on left, also a beach access road along the fence.

3 KM; 135.2 Miles (135.2S / 1.8N)
San Vincente trailer park.

0 KM; 137.0 Miles (137.0 S / 0.0N)
Cabo San Lucas.

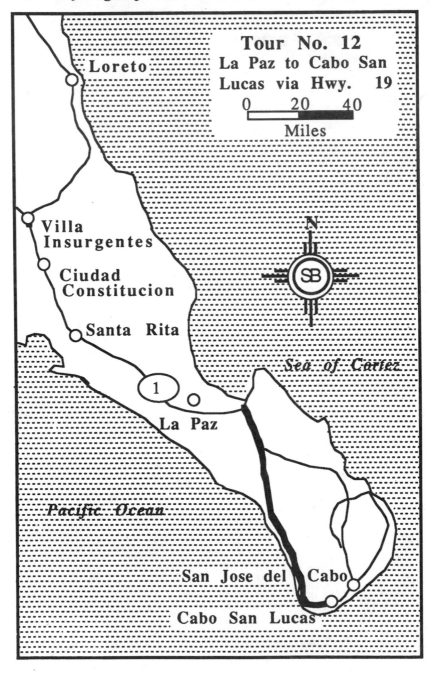

Tour No. 12
La Paz to Cabo San
Lucas via Hwy. 19
0   20   40
Miles

TOUR NO. 12 - CABO SAN LUCAS TO LA PAZ VIA HIGHWAY 19

Length: 163 KM / 101 Miles

Time Required: Two to three days

Season: October to April

Difficulty: Average

Most of the hills of this tour are at the beginning with steady climbing out of Cabo San Lucas. Reaching the Pacific near Migrino the road goes back inland and then parallels the coast to Todos Santos. Gentle, rolling hills out of Todos Santos are followed by a long gradual downhill back to La Paz.

General:

This tour describes the route from Cabo San Lucas back to La Paz via Highway 19. This tour may be combined with Tour No. 11 (La Paz to Cabo San Lucas via Highway 1) to form what has been called the Cape Loop trip. This loop trip makes an ideal one week tour with plenty of time to sample that which is still laid back Mexican in flavor and that which offers more tourist facilities than anywhere else on the peninsula. However, if your time is limited, Tour No. 12 in reverse provides the quickest route to Cabo San Lucas from La Paz. It is some 30 miles shorter than Tour No. 11 (and less developed) with some beautiful beach opportunities. Your decision as to which tour to take must be made by the time you reach the junction of Highways 1 and 19 near San Pedro, some 22 miles south of La Paz. The route descriptions of Tours 11 and 12 assume a clockwise traverse of the loop. However, I feel there is no advantage or disadvantage to either direction - I've experienced head winds and tail winds in both directions.

Point of Entry: Cabo San Lucas

Cabo San Lucas, though smaller than Cabo San Jose, has been transformed suddenly from a dusty, sleepy, friendly little village at the tip of the peninsula, into a bustling tourist mecca. While it is not a Mazatlan or Acapulco, people obviously love the place with approximately 250,000 tourists visiting there in 1987. Understandably, bicyclists love it too, especially those who have cycled the 1,059 miles from the border. For these, finding the KM 0 post across from the plaza is sometimes an emotional event, if even for only a moment or two.

The Cape Region with Cabo San Lucas as a central focus has indeed had a colorful history. Different groups of Indians have called it home. Pirates found the hidden bays and coves ideal hideouts from which to attack treasure-laden Spanish galleons. The conquistadores were followed by the missionaries, whose attempts at colonization were a long time in succeeding. Epidemics, hurricanes and the scarcity of food made the early days difficult. However, with one accomplishment after another, the taming of this desert peninsula has slowly been evolving. Today, aside from its first-rate hotels, resorts, fancy restaurants and quaint boutiques, there are still empty beaches and some pristine backcountry to be explored. If you have been exploring throughout your previous tours and feel it's time for some serious partying - this is the place.

Logistics:

Currently, Highway 19 has very little traffic and offers stimulating riding; however, there is no water available until Elias Calles nor food until El Pescadero. If you plan to stop at one of the beaches, take supplies. Public transportation to either Cabo San Lucas or La Paz is plentiful - by land (bus), sea, or air - as are the services necessary to the cyclist, in both cities.

Route Log:

The kilometer readings shown refer to those on kilometer posts along the route.

0.0 Miles (0.0 N / 101.1S; el. 10 ft.)
Junction of Highways 1 and 19 at Calle Matamoros (by the laundromat), **Cabo San Lucas.**

122 KM; 3.7 Miles (3.7N / 97.4S; el. 100 ft.)
Leaving town. Dirt road left to the new lighthouse. Still climbing.

119 KM; 5.6 Miles (5.6N / 95.5S)
Dirt road right to airport - no commercial flights.

115 KM; 8.0 Miles (8.0 N / 93.1S)
Road right to **Rancho San Ramon.**

113 KM; 9.3 Miles (9.3N / 91.8S)
Rancho Agua de Abajo to left. **Rancho El Mangle** to right.

111 KM; 10.5 Miles (10.5N/ 90.6S; el. 840 ft.)
Summit - last big view of Cabo San Lucas and the bay. Road starts downhill with views of the Pacific ahead. **Rancho La Palma** on way down.

108 KM; 12.4 Miles (12.4N / 88.7S; el. 300 ft.)
Road left. Begin uphill.

106 KM; 13.6 Miles (13.6N / 87.5S; el. 580 ft.)
Summit.

103 KM; 15.5 Miles (15.5N / 85.6S)
Road left to a new development - lots for sale.

102 KM; 16.1 Miles (16.1N / 85.0S)
Roads right and left - uphill.

101 KM; 16.7 Miles (16.7N / 84.4S)
Road right.

99 KM; 18.0 Miles (18.0 N / 83.1S)
Road right.

97 KM; 19.2 Miles (19.2N / 81.9S)
Most of the downhill is over and road swings right.

96 KM; 19.8 Miles (19.8N / 81.3S; el. 120 ft.)
Road left, which passes a house, then go right at the Y to
Migrino Beach - one of the nicest along this stretch.

94 KM; 21.1 Miles (21.1N / 80.0S)
Another road left to beach.

92 KM; 22.3 Miles (22.3N / 78.8S)
Roads right and left.

89 KM; 24.2 Miles (24.2N / 76.9S)
Top of climbing.

86 KM; 26.0 Miles (26.0 N / 75.1S)
Rancho Conejo to right.

82 KM; 28.5 Miles (28.5N / 72.6S)
Back to the beach. Access road with small house next to it.
Rancho El Paso and **Rancho Los Piedritas** on the left.

78 KM; 31.0 Miles (31.0 N / 70.1S)
Rancho Pinos - orchard on both sides of the road - well
water available.

75 KM; 32.8 Miles (32.8N / 68.3S)
Rancho Elias Calles. No services, just a cluster of houses
among the palms. There is a government water fixture on the
right next to the road - good drinking water. Shortly after the
houses is a road left which goes to a nice beach. Most of the
Pacific beaches along here are steep, with a strong undertow.
Use caution if you go into the surf. A 1 KM hill follows this
turnoff.

69 KM; 36.6 Miles (36.6N / 64.5S)
Several roads right to the beach for the next 3.1 miles.

62 KM; 37.2 Miles (37.2N / 63.9S)
Cafe on left.

61 KM; 41.5 Miles (41.5N/ 59.6S; el. 100 ft.)
El Pescadero - population 1500. A dirt road makes a sharp, right turn into town. You can see the town from the highway. It has limited groceries. A school and cafe face the plaza. A picturesque, small chapel is perched atop a hill overlooking town and the ocean. El Laurel Cafe and *deposito* are located on the highway.

58 KM; 43.4 Miles (43.4N / 57.7S)
Road left.

57 KM; 44.0 Miles (44.0 N / 57.1S)
Road left to **Playa San Pedrito**, across from the Forestry Experimental Station.

54 KM; 45.9 Miles (45.9N / 55.2S)
Road left to **Punta Lobos**.

50 KM; 48.3 Miles (48.3N / 52.8S)
Todos Santos - population 6,000. This quiet and tropically picturesque town serves the local experimental farming and forestry community. Sugar cane and mangos are the major crops, with a small sugar cane mill just north of town. The plaza, with an interesting and uniquely styled mission, is one block west of the main dirt road through town. There is also a paved road through town which bypasses the main business street. Todos Santos has an excellent *panaderia* (great molasses cookies), a *tortilleria*, a big *abarrotes* (at the top of the hill entering town from the south), and two restaurants. A campground is located behind the Santa Monica Restaurant at the bottom of the hill. There is a bank, *correos*, medical clinic, a rustic hotel and even a bed-and-breakfast establishment. The Todos Santos Inn has three rooms available in a 135-year-old house located at 17 Obregon. There is a significant contrast between this conservative community and the towns on the Sea of Cortez side of the cape.

48 KM; 49.6 Miles (49.6N / 51.5S)
Restaurante El Paso.

45 KM; 51.4 Miles (51.4N / 49.7S)
End of fencing and homes.

42 KM; 53.3 Miles (53.3N / 47.8S; el. 600 ft.)
Road right to **Presa Santa Inez** (*presa* = dam).

41 KM; 53.9 Miles (53.9N / 47.2S)
Microondas.

37 KM; 56.4 Miles (56.4N / 44.7S)
Rancho with windmill on left.

35 KM; 57.6 Miles (57.6N / 43.5S)
Road left to **San Fueco de las Huertes.**

26 KM; 63.2 Miles (63.2N / 37.9S)
Road left to **Ramal Meliton Albanes.**

25 KM; 63.8 Miles (63.8N / 37.3S)
Road left to **Ejido La Matanza.**

24 KM; 64.5 Miles (64.5N / 36.6S; el. 820 ft.)
Road right to **El Pintado.**

21 KM; 66.3 Miles (66.3N / 34.8S)
Road left to **Santa Teresita.**

17 KM; 68.8 Miles (68.8N / 32.3S)
Road left to **San Martin and Palmarito de Abajo.**

15 KM; 70.0 Miles (70.0N / 31.1S)
Road right to **Los Cuatro Hermanos.** Fences from here to Highway 1 junction.

8 KM; 74.4 Miles (74.4N / 26.7S)
Club Carrizal. The building structure has been here for years, but I have never seen it in use. In 1987 the pool, grounds and play area were all cleaned up in possible preparation for campers. This remains to be seen.

3 KM; 77.5 Miles (77.5N / 23.6S)
Road left to **El Zorro y La Pina.**

0 KM; 79.4 Miles (79.4N / 21.7S; el. 760 ft.)
Junction with Highway 1. Follow Highway 1, 21.7 miles into
La Paz, as described in Tour No. 11 Route Log.

101.1 Miles (101.1N / 0.0 S)
La Paz.

**Reynaldo Reed on Highway 19 south of Todos Santos. The
Pacific Ocean side of the Cape Loop is still mostly
undeveloped and has fine beaches**

ROUGH STUFF (MOUNTAIN BIKE) TOURS

Baja provides one of the few remaining areas in a wilderness setting, easily accessible to north-of-the-border cyclists. This section consists of four tours, each of which may be traversed in a week or less. They provide the cyclist with backcountry or off-highway biking, varying in difficulty from average to rugged. The tours included are:

Tour No. 13 - Tecate - Laguna Hanson Loop

Tour No. 14 - San Felipe to Rancho Chapala

Tour No. 15 - Loreto Mountain Loop

Tour No. 16 - Cabo San Jose Dirt Loop

The tours may be taken separately or combined, depending on the amount of time and energy the cyclist has available. The four were combined into one excursion, called by the writer "The Baja 1000." A narrative description of that trip is included as an Appendix (see "We Tackle the Baja 1000," Appendix).

The tours described are negotiable by average, experienced riders. They do not require cache systems, or complex logistical support equipment, unless the cyclist so prefers. Remote family ranchos may be depended upon, in most instances, to provide water and food as necessary. One of the many unique things about these tours is that at this time there are people living in the Baja outback who have been untouched by tourism. Therefore, with food and water at crucial intervals, these journeys provide rare opportunities for easily accessible, uncomplicated, off-highway biking in a real wilderness environment.

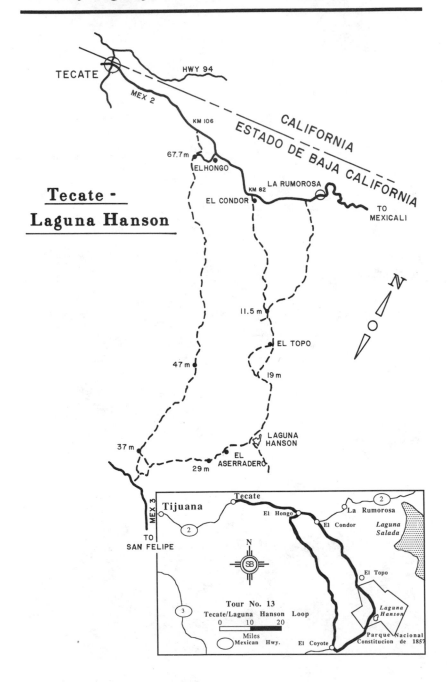

Tecate -
Laguna Hanson

Tour No. 13
Tecate/Laguna Hanson Loop

TOUR NO. 13 - TECATE / LAGUNA HANSON LOOP

Length: 109 miles on dirt, 53 on pavement (Highway 2), 163 miles total

Time Required: Five to seven days with a day at the lake

Season: April to December
A feature of this tour is that it can be taken from spring through fall (July and August can be hot) when most of Baja is "off season" for the cyclist. Most of the route is between 3,000 to 5,000 feet elevation, which can provide wonderful warm days, but chilly nights, in early spring and fall. I have been to Laguna Hanson in late November and found the nights very cold (frozen water bottles).

Difficulty: Average
This tour makes a very good first-time Baja mountain biking outing. The roads provide relatively easy riding. Keeping on the main road is easy, using appropriate maps. The most difficult part of the tour may well be the climb out of Tecate, on Highway 2, to the dirt road turnoff.

General:
Laguna Hanson lies southeast of Tecate in Parque Nacional Constitucion de 1857. This park is one of Baja's two northern national parks. The small, shallow, boulder-studded lake within the park is called Laguna Hanson and the whole park is often referred to as such. This tour forms a loop from Tecate to Laguna Hanson and return by a different route to Tecate.

The tour is not what most people would envision a trip to Baja to be. There are huge pine trees, alpine meadows, stream crossings, a lovely lake and frequent ranchos along the route. If time allows, there is a trail around the lake which provides a nice side trip. A rancho meal at Aserradero gives the trip additional flavor.

Point of Entry: Tecate

The city of Tecate lies 35 miles due east of Tijuana on Mexico Highway 2. The city is described in Tour No. 2 - Tecate to Mexicali.

Logistics:

If you have access to private transportation, I suggest getting a ride all the way to the turnoff at El Condor, east of Tecate. You will miss considerable hill climbing. Good bus service exists between San Diego, the major cities of Northern Baja, and Tecate (see Chapter 2, Logistics, Public Transportation). Suggested equipment for this tour is described in Chapter 2, Logistics, Equipment and Procedures.

Route Log:

Distances shown for this tour are in miles. It is assumed that this loop tour will be performed in a clockwise direction, starting toward the east. Therefore, elapsed miles are referred to as xxxE. The tour can also be taken in the counter-clockwise direction, hence the designator, xxxW.

0.0 Miles (0.0E / 162.5W)
Proceed east out of **Tecate** on paved Highway 2.

31.6 Miles (31.6E / 130.9W)
Turn right on dirt road at abandoned **El Condor** *loncheria* (KM 82). There are no Laguna Hanson signs. The dirt road has a good, hard-packed surface and starts off relatively flat, the area having gained elevation after leaving Tecate. Dirt road miles are referenced from the junction of the dirt road and Highway 2, at El Condor.

0.6 M; 32.2 Miles (32.2E / 130.3W)
Stay right at Y.

3.2 M; 34.8 Miles (34.8E / 127.7W)
Rancho on right with well.

9.9 M; 41.5 Miles (41.5E / 121.0 W)
Several ranchos up to this point.

11.6 M; 43.2 Miles (43.2E / 119.3 W)
Left at Y.

12.3 M; 43.9 Miles (43.9E / 118.6 W)
Right at Y.

15.3 M; 46.9 Miles (46.9E / 115.6W)
Stream at bottom of short steep hill - nice rest, or lunch spot. Also a stream crossing just beyond this, wide but very shallow.

18.4 M; 50.0 Miles (50.0E / 112.5W)
Corn garden on left.

18.5 M; 50.1 Miles (50.1E / 112.4W)
Road comes in on left from **La Rumorosa** (another starting point for this tour).

19.4 M; 51.0 Miles (51.0 E / 111.5W)
Left at T junction. There is a small sign for Laguna Hanson.

21.4 M; 53.0 Miles (53.0 E / 109.5W)
Road levels out after some climbing - good camping spots among the tall pines.

22.8 M; 54.4 Miles (54.4E / 108.1W)
Y - large meadow on right of **El Topo Rancho.** We went RIGHT here and the log details this (see "We Tackle the Baja 1000," Appendix). Would recommend going LEFT instead, for a better road than what we found to the right.

23.4 M; 55.0 Miles (55.0 E / 107.5W)
Water at El Topo if needed. Be sure to close gate.

24.0 M; 55.6 Miles (55.6E / 106.9W)
Sandy wash where road disappears for a short distance. Walk your bike up the super steep hill (0.5 miles). Road very faint. Evidently it is not used anymore.

25.8 M; 57.4 Miles (57.4E / 105.1W)
Top of hill. Gate.

29.8 M; 61.4 Miles (61.4E / 101.1W)
Left, at T junction.

30.7 M; 62.3 Miles (62.3E / 100.2W)
Road comes in from left - this would be the road from El Topo
if you kept left there. Much better condition.

34.5 M; 66.1 Miles (66.1E / 96.4W)
Left at Y to **Parque Nacional Constitucion de 1857.**
Road improves and is fast riding.

39.0 M; 70.6 Miles (70.6E / 91.9W)
Laguna Hanson.   Several campsites on the lake, last ones
have garbage cans and an outhouse.   Lovely setting, which
seldom has any visitors. Lake very shallow, lined with very
impressive, large boulders.

43.7 M; 75.3 Miles (75.3E / 87.2W)
Aserradero.   A small lumber village now nearly deserted.
Houses are made of wood from the mill. First house on left
will serve a meal (has a 7-Up sign on wall) and has a well
where you can get water. Turn right, out of the village.

46.8 M; 78.4 Miles (78.4E / 84.1W)
Right at Y (LEFT here to continue south to Highway 3 and on
to **San Felipe**).

52.1 M; 83.7 Miles (83.7E / 78.8W)
Road right.

56.4 M; 88.0 Miles (88.0E / 74.5W)
Right at Y.

58.8 M; 90.4 Miles (90.4E / 72.1W)
Rancho El Coyote on right. A road goes left.

59.4 M; 91.0 Miles (91.0E / 71.5W)
Right. Starts up hill immediately. The turn is shortly before a
cattle guard.

59.6 M; 91.2 Miles (91.2E / 71.3W)
Left at Y.

60.5 M; 92.1 Miles (92.1E / 70.4W)
Left at Y.

59.6 M; 91.2 Miles (91.2E / 71.3W)
Left at Y.

60.5 M; 92.1 Miles (92.1E / 70.4W)
Left at Y.

60.6 M; 92.2 Miles (92.2E / 70.3W)
Left at Y.

60.8 M; 92.4 Miles (92.4E / 70.1W)
Small road right.

60.9 M; 92.5 Miles (92.5E / 70.0 W)
Small road left.

61.6 M; 93.2 Miles (93.2E / 69.3W)
Top of a hill.

63.3 M; 94.9 Miles (94.9E / 67.6W)
Stream crossing at bottom of hill. A great spot with shade trees, running water (not drinkable). Leaving, the road makes a long, gradual climb.

64.4 M; 96.0 Miles (96.0 E / 66.5W)
Cattle guard. These occur frequently from here to Highway 2. Also there are occasional fences near the ranchos.

65.0 M; 96.6 Miles (96.6E / 65.9W)
Small road right.

66.7 M; 98.3 Miles (98.3E / 64.2W)
Small road left. Still more up than down.

69.6 M; 101.2 Miles (101.2E / 61.3W)
Rancho on left. Area has live oak trees, blue ceanothus (mountain lilac) and white mountain mahogany bushes.

70.2 M; 101.8 Miles (101.8E / 60.7W)
Cross a wash. Start roller coaster hills (short ups and downs).

72.6 M; 104.2 Miles (104.2E / 58.3W)
Road left.

73.7 M; 105.3 Miles (105.3E / 57.2W)
Nice campsite in trees.

Colin Warner and Mary Sinclair on a dirt road in Northern Baja

74.1 M; 105.7 Miles (105.7E / 56.8W)
Road right to **Casa Verde**.

75.0 M; 106.6 Miles (106.6E / 55.9W)
Cross a wash.

75.8 M; 107.4 Miles (107.4E / 55.1W)
Right at Y. Sign here for various ranchos. **San Juan de Dios** to the left - that road rejoins further north. **San Faustino and El Compadre**, stay right.

76.9 M; 108.5 Miles (108.5E / 54.0 W)
Highest summit, 4,540 feet. Grand vista.

78.8 M; 110.4 Miles (110.4E / 52.1W)
Can see a lake to the north.

80.4 M; 112.0 Miles (112.0E / 50.5W)
Stay RIGHT after cattle guard.

80.8 M; 112.4 Miles (112.4E / 50.1W)
Road from **San Juan de Dios** comes in on left.

81.9 M; 113.5 Miles (113.5E / 49.0W)
Windmill with water tank. Push on the float for water.

82.1 M; 113.7 Miles (113.7E / 48.8W)
Cross meadow. In April this was covered with a carpet of yellow flowers.

83.2 M; 114.8 Miles (114.8E / 47.7W)
Rancho.

84.0 M; 115.6 Miles (115.6E / 46.9W)
Cattle guard. Camping in the pines. More definite downhill now.

85.8 M; 117.4 Miles (117.4E / 45.1W)
Road left.

88.6 M; 120.2 Miles (120.6E / 42.3W)
Road right. Fences end.

93.9 M; 125.5 Miles (125.5E / 37.0W)
Road right. Across another wash with water.

94.1 M; 125.7 Miles (125.7E / 36.8W)
Left at Y. Rancho.

94.8 M; 126.4 Miles (126.4E / 36.1W)
Left at Y, top of hill.

95.0 M; 126.6 Miles (126.6E / 35.9W)
Campsite under some trees and in clearing further on.

95.6 M; 127.2 Miles (127.2E / 35.3W)
Road right.

96.9 M; 128.5 Miles (128.5E / 34.0 W)
Start more roller coaster hills.

97.8 M; 129.4 Miles (129.4E / 33.1W)
Top of a hill, steep and rutted downhill.

101.5 M; 133.1 Miles (133.1E / 29.4W)
Road left.

102.0 M; 133.6 Miles (133.6E / 28.9W)
Rancho on left, sells *queso* (cheese)!

102.2 M; 133.8 Miles (133.8E / 28.7W)
Road right.

102.3 M; 133.9 Miles (133.9E / 28.6W)
Rancho on left.

102.6 M; 134.2 Miles (134.2E / 28.3W)
Cemetery.

104.6 M; 136.2 Miles (136.2E / 26.3W)
Right at Y. Road rejoins in 0.4 miles.

105.8 M; 137.4 Miles (137.4E / 25.1W)
Rancho on right.

106.2 M; 137.8 Miles (137.8E / 24.7W)
Road left.

107.9 M; 139.5 Miles (139.5E / 23.0W)
Road left to **Hacienda Santa Veronica.**

109.0 M; 140.6 Miles (140.6E / 21.9W)
Pavement. **Rancho Los Javiers.**

109.1 M; 140.7 Miles (140.7E / 21.8W)
The pavement goes RIGHT to **El Hongo** on Highway 2, at KM 98, in 4.0 miles.

113.1 M; 144.7 Miles (144.7E / 17.8W)
Join Highway 2 at El Hongo, KM 98.

162.5 Miles (162.5E / 0.0W)
Travel west (LEFT) 17.8 miles on Highway 2 to **Tecate,** which completes the loop.

Still a good road by Baja standards

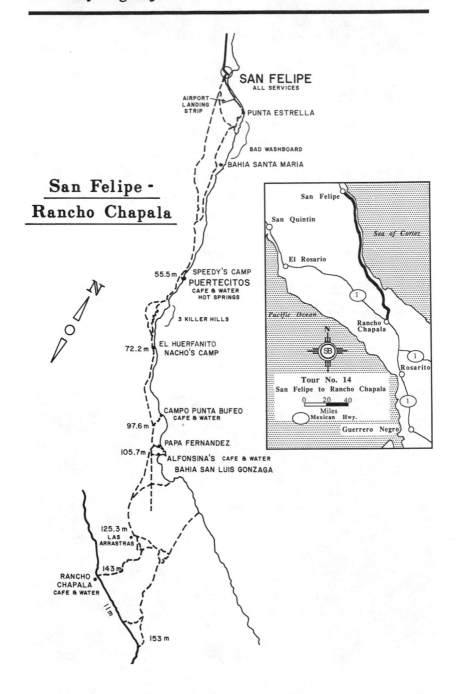

San Felipe - Rancho Chapala

SAN FELIPE
ALL SERVICES

AIRPORT
LANDING
STRIP

PUNTA ESTRELLA

BAD WASHBOARD

BAHIA SANTA MARIA

55.5 m SPEEDY'S CAMP
PUERTECITOS
CAFE & WATER
HOT SPRINGS

3 KILLER HILLS

72.2 m EL HUERFANITO
NACHO'S CAMP

CAMPO PUNTA BUFEO
CAFE & WATER

97.6 m

PAPA FERNANDEZ

105.7m ALFONSINA'S CAFE & WATER
BAHIA SAN LUIS GONZAGA

125.3 m
LAS
ARRASTRAS

143 m

RANCHO
CHAPALA
CAFE & WATER

11 m

153 m

San Felipe

San Quintin

Sea of Cortez

El Rosario

1

Pacific Ocean

Rancho
Chapala

SB

1

Rosarito

Tour No. 14
San Felipe to Rancho Chapala

0   20   40

Miles

Mexican Hwy.

1

Guerrero Negro

TOUR NO. 14 - SAN FELIPE TO RANCHO CHAPALA

Length: 140 miles on dirt, 10 on pavement, total, 150 miles

Time Required: Six to eight days

Season: November through February
Because of the distances between water sources, it is important to take this tour during mild weather.   With road improvements, there may well be more "traffic" to beg water from.   However, I would not count on it yet, especially from **Puertecitos** to **Bahia Gonzaga.**

Difficulty: Rugged
This tour follows a route along the **Sea of Cortez** coast starting at **San Felipe.**   It then turns southwest to intersect Highway 1 at **Rancho Chapala.**   The reputation of this route is currently being threatened by road builders blasting and grading to their heart's content, bent on "improving" the notoriously known "worst road in Baja."   Developers have had their eyes on this untouched stretch of coastline for a long time and roadwork finally got underway in 1985.   My friends who have recently traversed the road assure me that it will still remain a very challenging bike tour and to come prepared as there are no "facilities" looming on the horizon.   Consider this one if you have had some previous rough stuff experience.

General:
The highlights of this tour have been its sheer ruggedness and the challenges it presented.   After completing this tour you should feel (and know) you can ride anything!   Undoubtedly, whatever development eventually goes in will be along the beach. However, the terrain along this route, characterized best as extremely rugged desert wilderness, will probably remain untouched.

Point of Entry: San Felipe

San Felipe is found in Northern Baja on the Sea of Cortez coast. The city is described in Tour No. 4 - San Felipe to Ensenada.

Logistics:

San Felipe can be reached by bus out of Mexicali, or you can add 1 to 2 days and bicycle the 125 miles on the flat paved road. There is also bus service between Tijuana and Mexicali. When the dirt road meets the paved road at **Rancho Chapala** on Highway 1, you are in the middle of nowhere. Guerrero Negro is the closest town of any size and it is 110 miles south. You can, however, wait at the rancho and flag down a bus. The bus will stop and pick you up if they can fit your gear into the luggage compartment. It is also very easy to simply hitch a ride. There are many trucks on this section of Highway 1. Suggested equipment for this tour is described in Chapter 2, Logistics, Equipment and Procedures.

Route Log:

Distances shown for this tour are in miles.

0.0 Miles (0.0 S / 144.0 N)
Leave **San Felipe** on the paved road toward the airport.

7.4 Miles (7.4S / 136.6N)
Left at sign for **Laguna Chapala** (a right will go past the airport and on to the old road to Puertecitos. This is not a washboard road, but it is sandy in places).

10.0 Miles (10.0 S / 134.0 N)
Pavement ends. The road is heavily washboarded to **Puertecitos.**

11.3 Miles (11.3S / 132.7N)
Faro Beach turnoff. Trailer and camping park.

12.8 Miles (12.8S / 131.2N)
First of several roads to the beach, many are marked with signs. The beaches have varying degrees of camping facilities available.

15.2 Miles (15.2S / 128.8N)
Punta Estrella turnoff.

20.0 Miles (20.0S / 124.0 N)
Laguna Percebu (3 KM).

26.4 Miles (26.4S / 117.6N)
Bahia Santa Maria (1 KM)

30.0 Miles (30.0S / 114.0 N)
Campo La Perlita.

37.0 Miles (37.0 S / 107.0 N)
Campo Viviano (close to beach and deserted fish camp).

40 Miles (40.0S / 104.0 N)
Old road from San Felipe comes in on the right.

54.0 Miles (54.0 S / 90.0 N)
Speedy's Camp, upon reaching Puertecitos. Usually has drinks, sometimes a few groceries.

55.5 Miles (55.5S / 88.5N)
Puertecitos is a small village on the bay and is cluttered about with rundown trailers. These are occupied, for the most part, by Americans. On entering town, the house on the right carries a few groceries. At the Pemex turn left and follow the road out to the point. The sidewalk on the left leads to the beach, which features hot springs, exposed at low tide. There is a good cafe across from the Pemex. You can purchase water at a building which is up the hill and behind the Pemex. Ask at the cafe for the house that makes tortillas. Take some with you.

55.9 Miles (55.9S / 88.1N)
Continue south out of town and up the hill on the new graded road.

56.0 Miles (56.0S / 88.0 N)
Top of small hill. Road continues through coastal hills, up and down.

61.8 Miles (61.8S / 82.2N)
Leave coast and proceed inland. Sections of the old road may be seen toward the ocean.

66.3 Miles (66.3S / 77.7N)
Top of small hill then downhill.

66.7 Miles (66.7S / 77.3N)
Turn-off area with a small shrine. Good ocean view from here.

66.8 Miles (66.8S / 77.2N)
Bottom of hill. **El Huerfanito** can be seen.

67.3 Miles (67.3S / 76.7N)
Road left to Camp Chula Vista. Rolling, coastal road in this area.

68.4 Miles (68.4S / 75.6N)
Uphill.

69.1 Miles (69.1S / 74.9N)
Top of hill. Rolling, coastal road continues.

69.7 Miles (69.7S / 74.3N)
View of old road across arroyo. Begin uphill.

70.0 Miles (70.0S / 74.0 N)
Top of hill. Old road immediately to the left. Top of one of the sisters.

71.0 Miles (71.0S / 73.0 N)
Flat to slightly downhill.

71.4 Miles (71.4S / 72.6N)
Another sister. Downhill.

72.2 Miles (72.2S / 71.8N)
Last sister visible to right. Downhill to beach community (several houses, no facilities).

72.8 Miles (72.8S / 71.2N)
Bottom of hill. Start a short uphill.

73.2 Miles (73.2S / 70.8N)
Top of hill. Downhill slightly rough.

80.1 Miles (80.1S / 63.9N)
Rock house. Nice place for lunch.

83.1 Miles (83.1S / 60.9N)
Start uphill. Okies' Landing.

83.3 Miles (83.3S / 60.7N)
Top of hill.

83.7 Miles (83.7S / 60.3N)
Access road to beach.

84.8 Miles (84.8S / 59.2N)
Small beach to left.

85.9 Miles (85.9S / 58.1N)
Road right.

91.6 Miles (91.6S / 52.4N)
Road left.

93.9 Miles (93.9S / 50.1N)
Road left.

95.7 Miles (95.7S / 48.3N)
Road left (Camp Encantadas one mile).

97.3 Miles (97.3S / 46.7N)
Road left. Punta Bufeo.

97.6 Miles (97.6S / 46.4N)
Road left to **Punta Bufeo Beach**.   Inland, road passes
through small hills.

105.7 Miles (105.7S / 38.3N)
Alfonsino's turn off.

119.9 Miles (119.9S / 24.1N)
Rolling, uphill.

122.1 Miles (122.1S / 21.9N)
Top of gradual uphill.

125.3 Miles (125.3S / 18.7N)
Rancho to right. Las Arrastras, road working camp.

125.4 Miles (125.4S / 18.6N)
KM marker on road - KM 6.

129.5 Miles (129.5S / 14.5N)
Major road to left. KM marker on road - KM 0.

132.7 Miles (132.7S / 11.3N)
Begin uphill.

133.3 Miles (133.3S / 10.7N)
Top of hill. Begin downhill.

133.6 Miles (133.6S / 10.4N)
Start uphill (KM14 marker).

135.7 Miles (135.7S / 8.3N)
Top of hill. Begin downhill.

136.0 Miles (136.0 S / 8.0 N)
Start uphill.

137.0 Miles (137.0 S / 7.0 N)
Top of hill.

143.0 Miles (143.0 S / 1.0 N)
Junction, Highway 1. Turn south on Highway 1.

144.0 Miles (144.0 S / 0.0 N)
Rancho Nuevo Laguna Chapala. Cold drinks, food.

Mountain Villages Loop

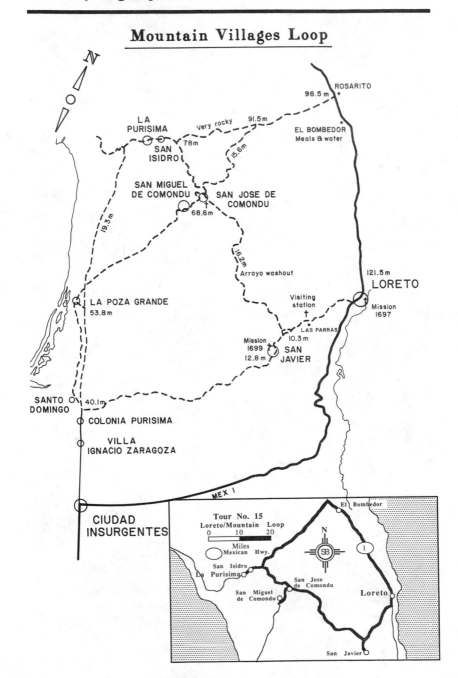

TOUR NO. 15 - LORETO / MOUNTAIN LOOP

Length: 135 miles on dirt, 38 on pavement, 169 miles total

Time Required: Six to seven days

Season: November into March
At an average elevation of approximately 2,000 feet, the weather can be cool in December and January. It can also be warm at any time.

Difficulty: Difficult to Rugged
Generally, this route borders on moderate difficulty to challenging. This is due to several short, steep hills that require walking the bike. Food and water, however, are available at regular intervals. The backcountry roads are generally in good riding condition, but there are some very rocky stretches and a few short, sandy stretches.

General:
This tour forms a loop starting at **Loreto** on the Sea of Cortez coast in Baja California Sur. The route swings southwest just south of Loreto, then loops northward through the Sierra de la Gigantia range. Often called "The Mountain Villages Tour," the route passes through the mountain villages of **San Javier, San Jose de Comondu, San Miguel de Comondu, La Purisima, and San Isidro.** Finally, heading northeast out of San Isidro, it links up with Highway 1 about 35 miles north of Loreto and returns there.

To me this is Baja mountain biking at its best. It represents perhaps the best combination of scenic, rugged and challenging road riding yet offered. In addition, the tour affords opportunities to visit remote, non-tourist oriented communities of quiet, shy and friendly people.

Point of Entry: Loreto

Loreto lies some 700 miles southeast of Tijuana on the Sea of Cortez coast. The city is described in Tour No. 10 - Loreto to La Paz.

Logistics:

Good transportation connections help to make this a popular tour. Loreto has both bus and air service from Tijuana and also air service from Los Angeles (see Chapter 2, Logistics; Public Transportation). The loop can be traversed in either direction. I follow the route in the clockwise direction, which leaves the option of shortening the route out of the Comondus, if time runs short. Suggested equipment for this tour is described in Chapter 2, Logistics; Equipment and Procedures.

Route Log:

Distances shown for this tour are in miles.

0.0 Miles (0.0S / 168.6N)

The tour begins at the **Loreto** plaza. Leave town and turn south on Highway 1 toward the airport. There is a road sign for **San Javier** approximately 3 miles from the Loreto plaza and 0.5 miles before   the airport turnoff. Turn right for San Javier.

6.5 Miles (6.5S / 162.1N)

Easy riding through rolling hills toward the impressive Sierra de la Gigantia range. First large,   wide,   dry arroyo encountered here. A good place to camp if you started late from Loreto.

9.0 Miles (9.0 S / 159.6N)

Arroyo with running water. Rancho and goats. Up and down terrain (mostly up), several arroyos with water, for the next 2 miles. At approximately mile 10, a pool with palms is to the right at some distance. Another arroyo, then steady climbing with terrific views back toward the Sea of Cortez with its sparkling shoreline.

14.0 Miles (14.0 S / 154.6N)
Rancho Las Parras and a small chapel. Some groves of oranges and olives, also a well. This is almost at the top of the climb. The road levels off here and has several water crossings.

22.0 Miles (22.0 S / 146.6N)
Big pool for swimming on right.

23.3 Miles (23.3S / 145.3N)
Somewhat rocky road with slight downhill toward town.

26.0 Miles (26.0 S / 142.6N)
Enter San Javier. The mission tower comes into view first. This impressive mission, of Moorish style, is the second (Loreto first) of the Baja California's Jesuit missions. Founded in 1699, it was completed in 1758. It is still in use and is in excellent condition. Near the mission, Casa de Arce will serve a meal. You can buy oranges, when in season, from the kids. Senora Arce is also the mission keeper and has a key. She will open the mission for you if you wish to see inside. You can climb the spiral stairs to the bell tower. Antique church vestments in glass cases are on display. The town is nearly deserted (less than 200 residents) except for a grand fiesta, Dec. 1, 2, 3 - All Saints Day.

31.0 Miles (31.0 S / 137.6N)
Backtrack on the road you came in, past the "swimming hole." Look for an unmarked road LEFT to the Comondus. Watch carefully for the telephone line going left, which you will follow.

31.5 Miles (31.5S / 137.1N)
LEFT again with the telephone line. Sign for Loreto, 30 KM. This road goes straight to, and on, the old road. It is a smaller road than the previous one, but is hardpacked. There is a short up, then a steep down, with a continuing, gradual downhill grade. At the bottom is a dry arroyo with the bridge washed out, then a BIG UP. Be mentally ready to walk your bike up this hill. It is steep, rocky and long (2.5 miles).

46.0 Miles (46.0 S / 122.6N)

Almost at the top of the hill there is a relatively flat spot on the left. A great sunrise spot. At the top are two goat ranchos. These are followed by a big downhill with switchbacks, followed again by an uphill, then a flat, short run up, flat again, then a gradual, becoming steep, downhill to **San Jose de Comondu**. San Jose de Comondu is a date palm oasis located at the bottom of a canyon.

62.0 Miles (62.0 S / 106.6N)

Enter the villages of **San Jose de Comondu,** followed by **San Miguel de Comondu**. Upon entering the first village you will see houses on the left with beautiful flowers. Dates are sold at one of them. There are two stores (the best one is closest to the plaza) and you can get water at the plaza. Ask at the store which house will cook a meal. There are no cafes. On the left near the Plaza are the remains of a stone building belonging to the Jesuit mission, established in 1737. The bells date back to 1708. There is a *correo* across from the store. San Miguel also has a small store and a *cerveza deposito*. The verdant green valley in which these villages are located, is about 7 miles long, with steep canyon walls on both sides.

67.0 Miles (67.0 S / 101.6N)

Backtrack from San Miguel to San Jose and turn LEFT just before the main part of town. This lovely road, lined with tall palms, leads north.

67.2 Miles (67.2S / 101.4N)

Start steep uphill with two switchbacks.

68.1 Miles (68.1S / 100.5N)

Top of hill turn LEFT - pass cemetery on right.

71.0 Miles (71.0 S / 97.6N)

Camping possible on the left. There are no rocks, but it is close to the road. The area has seen considerable volcanic activity. The landscape is heavily covered by scattered, volcanic rock, making campsites difficult to locate.

84.0 Miles (84.0 S / 84.6N)

Follow a few short ups, then a gradual down, becoming a long, steep down. Good views of the palms and town at the summit.

86.0 Miles (86.0 S / 82.6N)

Enter villages of **San Isidro** followed by **La Purisima**. These form another set of small towns only three miles apart in a fertile, canyon valley. To me these two towns are more different than alike. After coming down the big hill into San Isidro, a suburban area appears. Located here are a store, water spigot and a school, then the main part of town is entered. The entrance road follows along beside a spring-fed canal. The town boasts two stores, *cerveza deposito*, water at

Loreto administrative building just off the town plaza. "Mother Mission" (1697) to left.

the plaza, a motel of sorts, a *correo* and a nice public plaza. We have obtained meals at the green painted house across from the store, nearest the plaza. Continue straight through town about three miles to reach the village of La Purisima, which is said to have the smaller population of the two towns.

La Purisima has spacious buildings, a divided parkway and some well-kept homes along the main road. Yet, the town seems barely alive for some reason. Whereas, goat herding and goat cheese making are the major industries of the Comondus and San Isidro, many of the people in La Purisima are fishermen and journey out to the coast to ply their trade.

94.0 Miles (94.0 S / 74.6N)
Backtrack through San Isidro to the base of the hill you came down from the Comondus. Turn LEFT on the good road you can see switchbacking up the hill (east). This is the major climb on the route to the paved road. It is steep at first then becomes more gradual. A rancho on a small pond of water provides a nice setting for lunch. From here the road is a very gradual downhill with some flat stretches and passes some abandoned ranchos (or seasonal farms). There are several Y's in the road, but their turnoffs generally rejoin at short distances further on.

122.0 Miles (122.0 S / 46.6N)
A definite road coming in on the right. This road goes to San Jose and San Miguel Commondu.

127.0 Miles (127.0 S / 41.6N)
After a downhill and then a flat run, an incredible stretch of boulders makes up the road bed. This is a real test of the bicycle - if you ride it. About three miles before the pavement begins, there is a nice, wide arroyo lined with *palo blanco* and *palo verde* trees.

133.0 Miles (133.0 S / 35.6N)
RIGHT at the junction with Highway 1, at 59 KM road marker.

136.2 Miles (136.2S / 32.4N)
Rancho Bombedor.   Good meals, also water from a well at 54 KM. Mostly rolling hills accompanied generally by a tail-wind on into Loreto.   There is a nice view of town from the last hill before descending back to sea level.

168.6 Miles (168.6S / 0.0 N)
Loreto.

Sonya Lorenz at post office in San Isidro

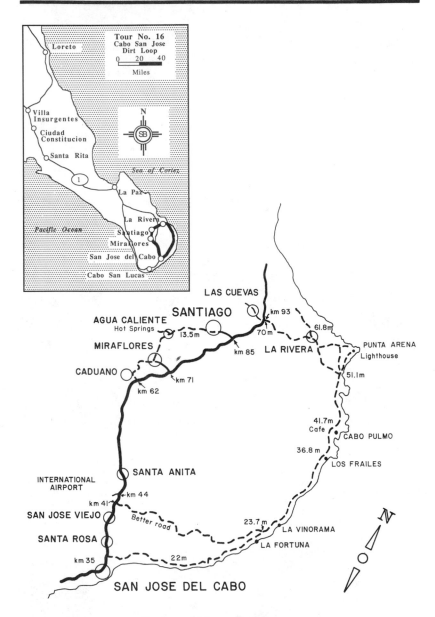

Cabo Dirt Loop

TOUR NO. 16 - CABO SAN LUCAS DIRT LOOP

Length: 87 miles on dirt, 32 miles on pavement, total, 118 miles

Time Required: Five to seven days

Season: November to March

It can be a very hot 90 degrees (F.) plus at any time, but this is more likely after March. It can be quite windy in January and February.

Difficulty: Average

The tour is very easy with no major climbs. However, though the terrain is easy, the coast road is often well washboarded, the bane of cyclists. Let a little air out of your tires and search for that elusive 6-inch wide, smooth belt.

General:

Perhaps the greatest draw to Baja is its famous beaches, especially those along the popular Sea of Cortez. The white sands between the two Cabos are rapidly being developed, yet north of San Jose del Cabo lie nearly 60 miles of coastline with direct beach access. This tour originates in San Jose del Cabo and proceeds north along this 60 miles of coastline to La Ribera. It then turns inland, crosses Highway 1 and passes through the villages of Santiago, Agua Caliente, Miraflores, and Caduano before returning to Highway 1. The route then follows Highway 1 back to San Jose del Cabo. The short dirt section between Santiago and Caduano is a fine example of what the inland roads have to offer. However, the elapsed time for this tour will depend on how many beach days you wish to spend.

Logistics:

This loop easily fits into a one week touring period and is made quite accessible with Los Cabos International Airport as the starting point. You can cut off some of the bad washboard by taking the road to the coast (22.3 miles) just south of the airport. Suggested equipment for this tour is described in Chapter 2, Logistics, Equipment and Procedures.

Route Log:
Distances shown for this tour are in miles.

0.0 Miles (0.0 N / 117.7S)
The tour begins at the Pemex station in **San Jose del Cabo**. Continue on the main road into town from the north, with the Pemex on your left. Follow the road down and up a hill. Along this road are several stores, a bank, hotel, Aero Mexico office, city plaza and other businesses. Just past the plaza is a stop sign. Turn RIGHT; road is divided with municipal buildings on the side.

1.1 Miles (1.1N / 116.6S)
LEFT on Benito Juarez, there is also a sign for Pueblo La Playa. Wide road, dense vegetation, crops.

2.2 Miles (2.2N / 115.5S)
Pueblo La Playa. LEFT at Y.   Right is to La Playita Restaurant/Bar.

2.4 Miles (2.4N / 115.3S)
Abarrotes Mary on right.

2.6 Miles (2.6N / 115.1S)
RIGHT at Y (keep on road with power poles).

2.7 Miles (2.7N / 115.0 S)
Conosupo in a house on the right.

2.8 Miles (2.8N / 114.9S)
Road to the right goes to a lighthouse. Road signs: Los Frailes 43 KM, Cabo Pulmo 51 KM, La Ribera 89 KM, Las Cuevas 100 KM. Kilometer post 0 is here. Road narrows and is badly washboarded.

3.8 Miles (3.8N 113.9S)
Rancho on left with livestock. Sea of Cortez in view.

4.1 Miles (4.1N / 113.8S)
Sand dunes on right.

4.2 Miles (4.2N / 113.5S)
White sandy beach, accessible by bike through undergrowth.

4.5 Miles (4.5N / 113.2S)
Nice beach.

5.2 Miles (5.2N / 112.5S)
Beach accessible via small trail.

5.5 Miles (5.5N / 112.2S)
Road to beach, also road above on a bluff.

5.7 Miles (5.7N / 112.0 S)
Road to beach.

6.2 Miles (6.2N / 111.5S)
Open beach accessible by bike. Kilometer post 59.

6.3 Miles (6.3N / 111.4S)
Car pullout on the road.

7.0 Miles (7.0 N / 110.7S)
Uphill away from beach. Small brush/cacti on both sides of road.

7.5 Miles (7.5N / 110.2S)
Road left.

8.3 Miles (8.3N / 109.4S)
Top of a hill with a clearing off to the right.

8.9 Miles (8.9N / 108.8S)
Top of another hill, beautiful coastline view. Road improves, but still washboard.

9.3 Miles (9.3N / 108.4S)
Kilometer post 90.

9.9 Miles (9.9N / 107.8S)
Roads left and right.

10.5 Miles (10.5N / 107.2S)
Road close to beach again, more dry and barren dirt with little ground cover.

11.4 Miles (11.4N / 106.3S)
Rancho on left with well, road to beach on right.

11.7 Miles (11.7N / 106.0 S)
Road to beach.

12.4 Miles (12.4N / 105.3S)
Kilometer post 85. Beach access.

13.6 Miles (13.6N / 104.1S)
Beach access possible by bike.

13.8 Miles (13.8N / 103.9S)
Bottom of *vado* and beach access.

14.0 Miles (14.0 N / 103.7S)
Top of a hill, road on left. Very sandy.

14.1 Miles (14.1N / 103.6S)
Rancho on left, beach access on right.

14.4 Miles (14.4N / 103.3S)
Top of a hill, several houses and trailers on right.

14.5 Miles (14.4N / 103.2S)
Road to left.

15.4 Miles (15.4N / 102.3S)
Rancho Agueda on left.

15.7 Miles (15.7N / 102.0S)
Kilometer post 80.

15.8 Miles (15.8N / 101.9S)
Sandy arroyo to beach on right.

16.2 Miles (16.2N / 101.5S)
La Fortuna. Several houses on beach, palm trees, well. Steep climb away from the water. Fence on beach side, ground heavily brush-covered on left.

17.2 Miles (17.2N / 100.5S)
Rancho Las Destiladeras, road right. Fence ends, monument on point.

18.3 Miles (18.3N / 99.4S)
Rancho Boca de las Palmas on left.

19.1 Miles (19.1N / 98.6S)
Top of a hill. Rock monument on right. Governor of State of Baja Sur dedicated the road to rural people, May 1984. Road improves, but more hills.

19.9 Miles (19.9N / 97.8S)
Rancho Santa Elena on right, on beach with palms.

20.2 Miles (20.2N / 97.5S)
Bottom of *vado*, beach access, lots of sandstone.

20.4 Miles (20.4N / 97.3S)
Huge tree for shade beside the road.

21.0 Miles (21.0N / 96.7S)
Rancho San Luis, quite meager.

21.1 Miles (21.1N / 96.6S)
Rancho on right, road goes inland, some cardons, some sandy spots with hills.

21.9 Miles (21.9N / 95.8S)
Road left.

23.0 Miles (23.0 N / 94.7S)
Kilometer post 70.

23.7 Miles (23.7N / 94.0 S)
Big road left, goes back to San Jose Viejo (and San Jose del Cabo airport).

23.8 Miles (23.8N / 93.9S)
Beach access and houses.

23.9 Miles (23.9N / 93.8S)
Well on right.

24.0 Miles (24.0 N / 93.7S)
Rancho Boca de las Vinoramas on right, has a big house, well.

24.8 Miles (24.8N / 92.9S)
Bottom of *vado*, beach access right.

26.1 Miles (26.1N / 91.6S)
Rancho on right, road uphill and inland.

27.8 Miles (27.8N / 89.9S)
Rancho on right.

29.0 Miles (29.0 N / 88.7S)
Downhill and closer to beach again, sandy for 0.2 miles.

29.4 Miles (29.4N / 88.3S)
Rancho Boca del Salada on right, trees, horses, well. Uphill and away from water.

30.4 Miles (30.4N / 87.3S)
Sand dunes to right, thick vegetation.

31.0 Miles (31.0 N / 87.7S)
Top of a hill, good road right.

31.3 Miles (31.3N / 86.4S)
Kilometer post 60.

32.9 Miles (32.9N / 84.8S)
Road to beach, 0.5 miles. Washboard again.

34.4 Miles (34.4N / 83.3S)
Nice house on left.

34.8 Miles (34.8N / 82.9S)
Road left, Kilometer Post 55.

35.5 Miles (35.5N / 82.2S)
Road left, houses on right, well.

35.7 Miles (35.7N / 82.0 S)
Road left.

36.1 Miles (36.1N / 81.6S)
Open clearing, road left.

36.2 Miles (36.2N / 81.5S)
Nice view of **Los Frailes.**

Reynaldo Reed takes a water break south of Todos Santos

36.7 Miles (36.7N / 81.0 S)
Lots for sale.

36.8 Miles (36.8N / 80.9S)
Well on beach side.   Several boats of local fishermen.
American RVs. This bay is part of a marine park that extends
north to **Cabo Pulmo.**

37.0 Miles (37.0 N / 80.7S)
Kilometer post 50. Road leaves beach and goes inland.

37.6 Miles (37.6N / 80.1S)
Rancho on left.

38.1 Miles (38.1N / 79.6S)
Nice view of mountains to the west.

38.8 Miles (38.8N / 78.9S)
Road right.

40.5 Miles (40.5N / 77.2S)
Road left. Small hills, nice rock formations.

41.1 Miles (41.1N / 76.6S)
Cement house on right, well.

41.5 Miles (41.5N / 76.2S)
Back to the water, several ranchos.

41.7 Miles (41.7N / 76.0 S)
Cabo Pulmo. Restaurant on left, nice shallow bay. Water is
warm.

41.9 Miles (41.9N / 75.8S)
Open beach area, steep climb away from beach.

43.7 Miles (43.7N / 74.0 S)
Road right. Kilometer post 40.

43.9 Miles (43.9N / 73.8S)
Thatched houses on right. Road is close to large, sweeping,
sandy beach.

44.5 Miles (44.5N / 73.2S)
Rancho las Barrancas, with trees and well.

44.9 Miles (44.9N / 72.8S)
Kilometer post 35. Road widens.

45.2 Miles (45.2N / 72.5S)
Several more houses.

46.1 Miles (46.1N 71.6S)
Short, steep hills. Several houses, well.

47.1 Miles (47.1N / 70.6S)
Road left.

48.0 Miles (48.0 N / 69.7S)
Fancy houses on beach side.

48.4 Miles (48.4N / 69.3S)
House on right.

49.0 Miles (49.0 N / 68.7S)
HUGE white hacienda on right.

50.0 Miles (50.0 N / 67.7S)
Kilometer post 30.

51.1 Miles (51.1N / 66.6S)
Y - these two roads rejoin 7.2 miles further down. Hardpacked landing strip here serving Hotel Colorado, approximately 4 miles to the right. LEFT to continue on to La Ribera.

58.3 Miles (58.3N / 58.8S)
The two roads of the 51.1 Y rejoin.

59.0 Miles (59.0 N / 58.7S)
Sandy stretch and washboard for about 1 mile.

60.0 Miles (60.0N / 57.7S)
Fields of agriculture, rancho on right, thick vegetation, few camping possibilities. Road improves.

61.0 Miles (61.0 N / 56.7S)
RIGHT at T to **La Ribera.**

61.3 Miles (61.3N / 56.4S)
Pemex on left, several houses.

61.8 Miles (61.8N / 65.9S)
La Ribera. *Cerveza deposito* off to the right, small market, cafe.

61.9 Miles (61.9N / 55.8S)
LEFT for the road west to Highway 1. Road is flat, some washboard sections past corn fields. Straight ahead will continue north to Buena Vista.

70.0 Miles (70.0 N / 47.7S)
LEFT at junction with Highway 1.

81.5 Miles (81.5N / 36.2S)
Kilometer Post 93.

82.7 Miles; 91 KM (82.7N / 35.0 S)
Start climb.

84.0 Miles; 89 KM (84.0 N / 33.7S)
Top of hill, few camping possibilities, rolling hills.

85.3 Miles; 85 KM (85.3 N / 32.4S)
Turn RIGHT 2 KM to **Santiago.** This small community has a nice plaza with reasonably stocked *abarrotes* (2), a *farmacia* and a cafe at the Hotel Palomar. The hotel is just off the plaza. Go straight after the first left around the plaza. This is the old road to Miraflores.

86.5 Miles (86.5N / 31.2S)
Santiago plaza. Note that the loop is now proceeding in a southerly direction, hence the change in mileage designators.

87.0 Miles (87.0 S / 30.7N)
Santiago church. RIGHT at T junction. Sign for zoo.

87.3 Miles (87.3S / 30.4N)
LEFT at T. Sign for zoo.

87.4 Miles (87.4S / 30.3N)
Zoo. Reasonable collection of Baja animals, reptiles and birds.

87.6 Miles (87.6S/ 30.1N)
Heavily washboarded section. Road right.

88.0 Miles (88.0 S/ 29.7N)
Kilometer post 1.

89.4 Miles (89.4S / 28.3N)
Road left.

90.6 Miles (90.6S / 27.1N)
Kilometer post 5.

90.9 Miles (90.9S / 26.8N)
Rancho and fields.

91.8 Miles (91.8S / 25.9N)
Kilometer post 7. Small village of **Agua Caliente.** School, *conosupo*. LEFT at Y and a sharp left at the corner house.

92.2 Miles (92.2S / 25.5N)
LEFT at Y and beehives. Sign for road right - Vinoramas.

93.4 Miles (93.4S / 24.3N)
LEFT at Y.

94.1 Miles (94.1S/ 23.6N)
Double gate and grate crossing (to keep the cows from wandering).

95.1 Miles (95.1S/ 22.6N)
Gate and grate crossing. Start up a hill, good road.

95.3 Miles (95.3S/ 22.4N)
Top of hill and shrine.

96.3 Miles (96.3S / 21.4N)
Roads left and right.

96.9 Miles (96.9S / 20.8N)
Rancho on left.

97.6 Miles (97.6S / 20.1N)
Miraflores. Town has school, *cerveza deposito*, telephone service, cafe and *mercado*. This town was once well known for its leather goods, for which you have to ask around to see now. The major commercial activities today are cheese making and fruit growing. At the plaza in Miraflores you can turn left, shortly after which the road becomes paved. It is 2 miles back out to Highway 1. To continue on to Caduano, proceed straight past the plaza.

99.1 Miles (99.1S / 18.6N)
LEFT at Y in the road.

100.0 Miles (100.0 S/ 17.7N)
Caduano.   Another small agricultural community nestled among spring fed trees.   Cafe and abarrotes.   LEFT for Highway 1.

101.0 Miles (101.0 S / 16.7N)
Highway 1 at Kilometer post 62.

110.3 Miles; 47 KM (110.3S / 7.4N)
Santa Anita.   Very small community along the highway. School and small *abarrotes*.

111.5 Miles; 45 KM (111.5S / 6.2N)
Road right.

112.2 Miles; 44 KM (112.2S/ 5.5N)
Airport road to the right; 2 KM to Los Cabos International Airport.

113.4 Miles; 42 KM (113.4S / 4.3N)
Road left.

114.0 Miles; 41 KM (114.0 S / 3.7N)
San Bernabe.   Church and *cervezeria*.   This road can also be used for starting this loop trip, if you are starting from the airport rather than from San Jose del Cabo.   It is about 23.8 miles from the junction at Mile 23.7 (shortly before Boca de la Vinoramas) on the route previously described.   By and large, this road is less washboarded and more interesting, with dense vegetation.   Also, it passes several ranchos and encampments where water and snacks may be obtained.

114.6 Miles; 40 KM (114.6S / 3.1N)
San Jose Viejo.   A growing residential community adjacent to San Jose del Cabo.   *Conosupo* and *mercado*.

115.9 Miles; 38 KM (115.9S / 1.8N)
El Zacatel. Houses and school.

117.1 Miles; 36 KM (117.1S / 0.6N)
Santa Rosa.   Another residential community with cafe and *mercado*.

APPENDICES

APPENDIX NO. 1

Spanish Terms Used In This Book

ABARROTES - A grocery store. They can be very limited, or can have a pretty good selection. In smaller places they may only have a few canned goods and no fresh foods. You won't starve, but you may have to stretch your imagination in creating a meal.

AGUA POTABLE - Potable water, i.e, water fit for human consumption.

ARROYO - A stream or river bed. In the case of Baja, they are usually dry unless heavy rains have occurred recently.

CAMPAMENTO - An encampment.

CARNITAS - A specialty when you can find them. Meat such as pork is sliced, or cut in cubes, and is served on a platter with avocados, tomatoes, beans and tortillas.

CORREO - A post office.

CERVEZA OR DEPOSITO - Beer, or a beer store.

CONASUPO - The government sponsored chain of grocery stores. Even the smallest village will have one. Again, there may be a very limited stock on hand.

EJIDO - This is a collection of families working common land usually for agricultural purposes. The land is owned by the *ejido* and is run by elected officials. They may or may not have any services.

FARMACIA - A pharmacy.

FONATUR - A tourist development agency.

I.M.S.S. - Instituto Mexicano de Seguro Social - medical services. They have radios for air evac 24 hour services out of San Diego, phone (619) 278-3822.

LIQUADOS - Often found at *paleterias,* they are sort of like milk shakes with a choice of fruits and sometimes nuts. Mixed in a blender with milk, juice, sugar, you'll be asked "con huevo" (egg)? Topped with cinnamon or other spices, they're delicious.

LONCHERIA - This is like a cafe. They are usually located in a town, but some Ranchos will use the word *"loncheria"* to indicate food is available.

MACHACA - Shredded meat - for burritos or mixed with eggs.

MERCADO - A market. It usually carries groceries also. Size doesn't seem to determine whether a store is a *mercado* or *abarrotes.* A supermercado, however, will have a much more extensive selection of goods.

MICROONDAS - A microwave radio phone system in southern Baja.

PALETERIA - A shop selling *paletas.* A *paleta* is like an old fashioned fruit popsicle only they leave in the fruit pulp with the blended juice and freeze it all on a stick. Usually there is a wide selection of flavors: strawberry, banana, cantaloupe, watermelon, pineapple, various types of nuts, etc. Those "con crema" are frozen with milk mixed in, giving a richer almost ice cream-like taste. Only in recent years have these become available in most Baja towns, primarily south of Guerrero Negro. A real taste treat! Yes, they use purified water and pasteurized milk. I stay away from strawberry, though.

PANADERIA OR PAN - A bakery, or bread.

PEMEX - The government petroleum company. It runs the gas stations.

PLAYA - A beach, usually with a public access road.

RAMAL - Commonly seen on the road signs. It just means a branch road to whatever is indicated on the sign.

RANCHO - Small, family run, self-sufficient or subsistent farm. Situated frequently along the highway, they often sell drinks, snacks, or meals to passersby. Having one meal a day at a rancho greatly reduces the amount of food to be carried between towns.

REFRESCOS - Pop or sodas.

SCT - Secretario Comunicacion Transportacion; pertains to functions of the office of the Secretary of Communication and Transportation

TIENDA - A store.

TORTILLERIA - You guessed it - where tortillas are made and sold. Usually very inexpensively, too. They are sold by weight rather than number. Making them is quite a fascinating procedure. The best place to see how the machinery works, and to get good photos too, is the public marketplace in Ciudad Constitucion.

TURISTA - Violent diarrhea sometimes suffered by tourists and usually blamed on the local Mexican food and water supplies.

VADO - A dip in the road.

APPENDIX NO. 2

We Tackle The Baja 1000

Preface

This narrative is based upon my road log and notes taken on a rough stuff, mountain bike tour in 1985. Our plan was to bike to La Paz through the backcountry, following many of the dirt roads and trails described in the Rough Stuff (Off - Highway) Tours section of this book. It is included here for the information of bikers who may be considering one or all of the aforementioned tours.

Introduction

It didn't take long to realize the storm that had been brewing for days was fast upon us. The sun was still high above the horizon but we quickly pulled off the road and hastily made camp. The distant rumble rapidly grew closer until loud, thunderous claps were crackling just overhead, with jagged streaks of light racing across the sky. The rain that followed was a real gully washer, pelting down hard, fast sheets of water. We couldn't even hear each other yelling across the twenty feet separating our tents.

At such times I begin to ask myself, is this fun? Really fun? I wonder why on earth I'm out there subjecting myself to a whole lot of hard work, not always having enough to eat, drinking a gallon and a half of water a day, only to urinate a quarter cup, and the constant anxiety of where the next water source will be. Then literally swamped in water inside the tent (so much for goretex), with the wind raging, besides thunder and lightning, I wasn't thinking about fun at all. It was just a little scary.

The storm confirmed what we had already concluded. October was not a good time of year to be doing a wilderness trip along the Sea of Cortez. We were trying to pick up our painfully slow pace to reach pavement and head on to the west side of the peninsula, hoping for cooler and more stable weather, to continue our pursuit of riding the dirt roads the length of Baja.

I - The High Desert (See Rough Stuff Tour No. 13 - Tecate Laguna Hanson Loop)

The first phase of the trip was in near perfect weather as we left Tecate and did some steady but gradual climbing to Parque Nacional Constitucion de 1857. The road to Laguna Hanson proved a joy to ride with very little walking.

With swimming and picture taking at the lake done, we rode on to Aserradero and had dinner with a local family. Our first rancho meal of eggs, beans, tortillas and sodas was one of the cheapest of the trip, $1.50 each, and dictated what was to be our prevalent diet for the rest of the month.

Gently descending from the mountains with numerous stream crossings, pine forests, open range of sage and chaparral and a skyline interrupted by various green, rocky hills in all directions, we hit upon the dry lake bed of Laguna Diablo. Here we found ourselves "speeding" through mirages at 20 mph on the cracked, hardpacked earth, invigorated by the stark and dramatic change in landscape. Feeling stronger, we were getting used to our heavily laden stumpjumpers loaded with minimal equipment, maximum water and whatever food we could buy along the way. Eating proved to be feast or famine throughout the trip and I began to realize how much this inconsistency of food intake was to affect my energy level.

Reaching San Felipe and some semblance of civilization, we enjoyed showers, a replete dinner, then renewed our food supply and 3 to 4 gallons of water apiece for the next and most arduous portion of the tour: down the Sea of Cortez to Laguna Chapala.

II The Sea of Cortez (See Rough Stuff Tour No. 14 - San Felipe to Rancho Chapala)

The ride to Puertecitos was a long, hot 50 miles, but we eventually made it to the outskirts of "town" by nightfall and on to the hot springs by moonlight. The soothing hot water amongst the beach rock pools gave us another one of those natural highs. There were certainly no doubts in my mind why I was doing what I was doing - riding the dirt roads to La Paz.

Our speed now dramatically diminished, not only because of the debilitating heat but the road itself was to teach us about real rough stuff. The next 50 miles to Bahia San Luis Gonzaga were to take three days to accomplish. This is some of the toughest Baja has to offer. There are steep hills, rocks and boulders to dodge, ruts deep and treacherous to wheels and occasionally soft sand that even brings fat tires to a halt.

On the other hand, the tough road reflected the awesome land it traversed, a beautifully rugged and untouched coastline. There was a certain magic to it all. We knew we were working even harder, yet, the energy flow and enthusiasm were heightened as the next rise always produced still another spectacular vista.

We continued riding until dark, then walked, by the moonlight, up the first of the three Killer Hills. We were all down to our underwear, as pushing the heavy bikes up the steep hill was hot work, even at night.

Our ninth day from Tecate dawned beautiful and clear, with good prospects to surmount the remaining two Killer Hills early, before it got too hot. It proved a disastrous day for both Marlene and Lynda. Marlene was very ill and extremely weakened. The best she could do was walk up the hills by herself, without the bike. By afternoon we reached the beach at Huerfanito and Leonardo and Lorene's cabin for shade, water, and relief at finding someone to help. We'd only come 5.6 miles on the route, but actually did several more miles up and down the hills with two people pushing each bike.

It was also discovered that Lynda's rear derailleur was broken. The prospect of riding a three-speed the rest of the trip wasn't very appealing and she wanted to help Marlene.

Mari and I reluctantly left to go south in the early morning. Our conversation was unenthusiastic and we finally confessed how much we missed the other two. The whole tempo was different.

We were pushing across a sandy arroyo when a four-wheel drive vehicle approached from the south. Being the first vehicle we'd met since Puertecitos it wasn't an annoyance. They had left La Paz that morning and had just turned onto the dirt road at Chapala a few hours before. That really made me straighten my back. La Paz was weeks away for us and they'd driven it in a day!

The following night the horrendous storm hit us before we could reach Rancho Chapala on Highway 1. The 150 miles from San Felipe took seven days.

III - The Pacific Side and Mountain Villages
(See Rough Stuff Tour No. 15 - Loreto / Mountain Loop)
We left San Ignacio in the afternoon, heading for the Pacific coast and Laguna San Ignacio, famous (in season) for gray whales. I was surprised at how many people were living along the beach in such dirty, little hovels. We bought sodas at one house and the man drew a map in the sand to give us directions south. There were roads from every direction and once again, the Baja map we had was useless.

The next day was one of the most worrisome of the trip. Mile after mile the road would fork and we had to determine which one to take. By afternoon we were in real doubt about our direction and how long we could go with the water we had left. With luck a truck, the first we'd seen in 26 hours, came by and told us Rancho Cuarenta was within two miles. This was the landmark we'd been looking for to confirm our position! At Cadeje we experienced a tremendous treat - fresh lobster dinners and all the trimmings we could eat. We astounded the watchful room full of people at how much we packed away. We ate ravenously but weren't embarrassed. Three young women managed the kitchen. We sat at the sole table acknowledging the many people who kept "dropping by" - - ostensibly to see the gringas. Every time someone entered this proper Mexican family home, they made their way around the room, with a handshake and embrace, even to the children. The children were well dressed, healthy looking, bright, polite and quite curious. The women were in very stylish dresses, making me shudder at my own shabby appearance.

We stopped at the store in San Juanico for a few supplies and found a terrific line. Fishermen were everywhere, buying 20 lb. bags of rice and beans for a month at sea. We really giggled over the mound of toilet paper one guy had stacked on the counter. Long ledger books were brought out to record each item and price, nothing high tech here.

La Purisima and San Isidro are sister villages about 3 miles apart. La Purisima had obviously looked toward bigger and better times in building the wide streets and center park-like dividers, typical of Mexico. There were large and substantially built buildings, but they held no businesses.

The next set of twins we visited were San Jose de Comondu and San Miguel de Comondu just two miles apart and also at the bottom of a palm studded canyon. Some children directed us to a house where we could purchase a meal. After a substantial meal, and not wishing to face another long uphill climb out of the canyon, we wondered if we might camp somewhere near. But it was as if the decision was already settled that we would sleep there. Our hostess, Consuelo, even had an empty room with two beds.

We left early, with Consuelo out in the street waving good-bye. It was a fine day of riding all the way to San Javier, the mission village, almost a ghost town.

Senora Arce (who is also the mission keeper) greeted us at her door and with proud ardor announced that she had eggs, beans and tortillas for us. Out back, Senor Arce was stirring a huge pot of guava candy over an open fire. He explained the process while the kids brought spoons so we could sample. Again, it was assumed we'd also be spending the night. So, we were shown our quarters - an unoccupied room next to the main house. This was half filled with cases of Tecate beer, for which the Arces obviously had the village franchise.

Upon approaching Villa Insurgentes, a truck stopped and the driver graciously offered us a ride. I didn't even look at Mari to see what she wanted to do and promptly accepted. Uppermost in my mind was a hot shower and clean clothes.

I'd "hit the wall" at being dirty! We hung out the back with grandpa, a flock of kids and a huge box of equipment and tools. Along with all this, the mountain bikes were squeezed in over the tailgate.

This was typical Baja style and we smiled with great satisfaction as we rode with our hosts not into Villa Insurgentes, but into Ciudad Constitucion. After accepting their hospitality we found out that Constitucion was their ultimate destination and the wheels in our minds started spinning. We had been in the back country for 24 days. We had hoped to be closer to La Paz. However, the extremely hot weather along the Sea of Cortez had slowed us down considerably. Nevertheless, we felt a form of elation in that we had lived on the edge of civilization, using only our own physical energy to make it.

We could spend four more days in Baja, then both of us had to get back to our "other worlds." On reaching Ciudad Constitucion with our truck full of friends, we concluded another 8 days and 160 more miles of Baja rough stuff. Our minds were made up. The next day we hitched a ride to La Paz and in three days spent more money than we had in the previous 25. Those three days were glorious, and though we hadn't quite biked our thousand miles of rough stuff, we had totaled over 1,000 kilometers - and that's a Baja mil!

APPENDIX NO. 3

Considerations for Potential Group Leaders and Others

If after reading "Bicycling Baja," you decide to give it a try, your first step will be to interest another cyclist in the notion. We have already mentioned that in most outdoor ventures - swimming, scuba diving, cross country skiing, whatever - the buddy system is the accepted, safe way to proceed. Never go it alone! If you are successful in interesting one other cyclist, the word will get around and the first thing you know, you have a group tour on your hands.   Great!   A group of mutually compatible cyclists can make a Baja tour a success, and best of all - fun.

Note the careful use of words - mutually compatible - for therein lies the problem. Furthermore, because all of this was your idea, you will more than likely wind up as group leader. Lots of luck!   We will assume you are technically and mentally equipped to lead Americans in cyclic combat, and will limit ourselves to a few comments concerning the American psyche - a mental makeup which can make or break a Baja trip.

Americans carry along a tremendous amount of emotional excess baggage when they travel.   It's easy to spot but certainly more difficult to ascertain why.   We all know the image portrayed by the Ugly American, loud, obnoxious and usually critical of everything non-American.

This is not in total defense of the Mexican culture or values. I can be just as patriotic as the next person. I love the United States and after living in a South American country for a year, I came to truly appreciate the privilege of living in the U.S. I just don't feel any inner need to flaunt my U.S. values in the faces of those whose country I'm visiting.   Understanding doesn't mean accepting, it just allows you to cope.

As to why some Americans go open-loop south of the border, is perplexing.   I'm sure there is plenty of expert documentation on the subject. From my observations it seems to boil down to lack of experience and insecurity. Often the combination of a first trip into a foreign country, coupled with a first multi-day bike trip, proves more stressful than anticipated.

A poor self-image, or insecurity, seems to be the other major emotional baggage carried into the foreign experience. Often it seems people overly critical of someone, or something else, may proclaim their own excellence on the surface, but deep down hold little confidence in the truth of such proclamations. Thus the braggart has little to brag about, or does so in a way that is offensive to others.

It's sometimes a fine line between the inexperienced and/or insecure person, coping with the foreign experience, and that of the maladjusted personality which manifests itself in what is called "culture shock." Fortunately, it doesn't happen often, but when it does, it's difficult to deal with and most certainly ruins a trip.

Occasionally people change personalities the minute they cross the border (Tijuana could certainly do it to anyone)! However, more often it's a culmination of many events and circumstances before a person reveals the telltale signs. Common characteristics include constant criticism of the trip, the people, the environment. Watch out for the normally good-natured person who becomes irritable with the slightest incident, touching off a tirade. Some totally withdraw and no longer contribute toward the goals of the trip, won't speak or interact with people along the way, or refuse new food, customs, etc. This person becomes genuinely miserable with the situation and soon makes everyone else uncomfortable. It's a sad situation because rational control over one's emotions is totally lost.

So how do you know if your trip south of the border is going to raise the unsavory aspects of someone's personality? I don't have a formula for a pre-trip diagnosis. However, certain characteristics provide good indications for a successful journey.

Someone who genuinely likes other people and is good at compromising makes a great traveling companion. In the case of Baja, I think a good appreciation of geography is also necessary since the peninsula is sparsely populated and towns can be some distances apart. I like the vast open space, simply meaning, an environment undeveloped and unencumbered by man's alterations. Others see it as empty space which holds nothing of interest. Liking people and the environment and possessing a little curiosity about each, seems a winning combination for enjoying a Baja journey.

There you have it. Hopefully, may you assemble that "mutually compatible" group, be blessed with a strong dose of good, American luck, and have a great one in Baja!

APPENDIX NO. 4

Excursions Within Baja

Cabo San Lucas - Perhaps the most famous landmark of all Baja is the rock arch where the Sea of Cortez and Pacific Ocean meet at Land's End. You can negotiate a trip at inexpensive rates with a panga driver at the docks, or go to the tourist dock and join a tour by Yates Fiesta Primavera. They offer 5 different trips for a 3-hour bay-and-arch excursion ($15.00), to a 6-hour cruise at $45.00.

Ensenada - Here is an opportunity to visit Baja's oldest winery. You can tour the Bodegas de Santo Tomas winery located on Avenida Miramar 666 at the corner of Calle 7. Tours cost $1.50 and are offered Monday through Saturday at 11 a.m., 1 p.m., and 3 p.m. It takes about half an hour and there is time for sampling afterwards.

Guerrero Negro - The current wave of whale mania has not been lost on one enterprising resident of Guerrero Negro. Mario Rueda offers whale watching trips by boat December, January, February and March. In February 1986 the charge was $20.00 for a cruise in Estero de San Jose from 9 a.m. to noon. We saw several whales and some at very close range. Mario's posters about the trip can be found at Malarrimo Restaurant and the Hotel Dunas in town. He comes to these places the evening before to take reservations. For those on bikes he will pick you up in his van in the morning.

La Paz - Several boat tours out of La Paz are available through an agency located at Los Arcos Hotel. I've found excellent service and value from the outfitter Reina Calafia, located at 220 Alvaro Obregon one block west of the Perla Hotel. There is usually a "sandwich board" type sign on the sidewalk. Juan Lopez offers half day boat tours to a deserted sandy beach for swimming and snorkeling (gear provided). He drives you to the launch site just past Pichilingue and returns you to the city afterwards. At $10.00 for the 4 - 5 hours, we found this an excellent tour.

San Ignacio - If you would like to visit the Palmarito Cave Paintings, or those at San Fransisquito, but don't have the requisite time, or mountain bike, there is a solution. A day or half day trip from San Ignacio is offered by Oscar Fisher, owner of the Posada Motel, several blocks off the square. It is an all day trip to Santa Marta, leaving promptly at daybreak and returning at sunset. He may impose a minimum number to go on these tours. A second trip, over a better road and taking less time, is to the cave paintings near Rancho San Francisco. This tour was $20.00 in the fall of 1987. Transportation is by pick-up truck.

Tecate - You can visit the famous Tecate Brewery from 8 a.m. to noon. Tours are given the first three Saturdays of each month. Call (706) 654-1202 for further information.

Note: all prices shown herein are per person and are subject to change.

APPENDIX NO. 5

Major Annual Baja Bike Fun-Rides & Tours

Fun-Rides
As many as 30,000 people participate in the various bike rides offered throughout Northern Baja. The events are highly organized and provide cyclists with an introduction to Baja. David Manwaring originated the rides in 1969. Their popularity has grown such that there is a significant impact of tourism on the town involved.

RIDE NO. 1 - ROSARITO - ENSENADA 50 MILE FUN BICYCLE RIDE

Contact:	Dave Dickson Bicycling West, Inc. P.O. Box 15128 San Diego, CA 92115 -0128 (619) 583-3001.
Year Began:	Annual Fall Ride began 1980 (uses a late September start date). Annual Spring Ride began 1987 (uses a mid-April start date).
The Ride:	The ride starts in Rosarito Beach some 17 miles south of Tijuana and covers 50 miles south to Ensenada. The route follows the coast before heading inland on the old road to Ensenada.
Structure:	Mass start event - no times. Open to individual riders and not teams.
Limit:	Currently no limit, no age limits, lots of families enjoy this ride. The rides draw 8,000 bikers in April, 13,000 in September. The two rides combined make this series the largest bicycle event in the world.

Cost:

$18.00 - Includes T- shirt, embroidered patch, emergency medical treatment and evacuation, if necessary. $6.00 - Bus return to Rosarito Beach (no bicycles!). $3.00 - For 5 x 7 color photo of group. $29.00 - For videotape of ride.

Promoter's Comments:
I tell people this ride is the equivalent of a 10 KM run. What makes this ride special is that it is a pleasant, uninterrupted, 50 mile ride, with no towns, or traffic lights in between, and very little traffic. We recommend people to have ridden a 50 mile ride previously. About 60% of the riders wear helmets. I would like to see more do so. Air-Evac of San Diego provides medical services.

Dave Dickson

RIDE NO. 2 - MEXICALI TO SAN FELIPE

Contact:

David Manwaring
Monday International, Inc.
P.O. Box 99120
San Diego, CA 92109
(619) 275-1384.

Year Began: 1979

Annual Date: The weekend before Halloween.

The Ride: The route from Mexicali to San Felipe is a very flat 200 KM / 120 Miles. This ride is for the rider with experience in distance riding. For a shorter ride, there is an official finish line at the 100 KM mark. Same services apply.

Structure: Mass start.

Limit: Currently no limit - the ride draws 1,500 - 2,000 riders.

Cost:	$15.00 - Includes aid stations, awards, fiesta at the end.

Promoter's Comments:
This ride is part of a series of rides conducted by Monday International. It's a rider's ride as the flatness can be tedious. It's a good challenge. We hope to provide a cycling event for everyone in the series.

David Manwaring

RIDE NO. 3 - BAJA COAST RIDE

Contact:	Victor Botello or Lowell Lindsay YMCA of San Diego County 7510 Clairemont Mesa Blvd. San Diego, CA 92111 (619) 423-9622 or 543-1060
Year Began:	1985
Annual Dates:	May - the first Sunday.
The Ride:	The ride from Tijuana to Ensenada is 65 miles. Government assistance is by the Mexico Federal Highway Department and State Department of Tourism. Because of this unique support, one lane of the beautiful Mexico 1-D (toll road) is opened to bikers for this special ride. This event offers the only opportunity for bikers to ride this scenic highway.
Structure:	Mass start.
Limit:	None imposed so far - will take up to 3,000.
Cost:	$15.00. Includes aid stations and T-shirt.

Promoter's Comments:
Currently, this is the only non-profit fun-ride event being staged in Baja. It is an international service project with proceeds to benefit YMCA projects on both sides of the border. TARGET Department Stores is the major support sponsor. We hope to see this event grow not only in the number of participants but also in the area of international cooperation and friendship.

Lowell Lindsay

RIDE NO. 4 - TECATE TO ENSENADA

Contact:	David Manwaring Monday International, Inc. P.O. Box 99120 San Diego, CA 92109 (619) 275-1384.
Year Began:	1969
Annual Date:	May. Scheduled after Mother's Day and before Memorial Day.
The Ride:	This ride from Tecate to Ensenada covers 72.8 miles of rolling hills and agricultural land. It is held during the International Sports Weekend sponsored by Monday International. On Saturday a run is held for 5 person relay teams. On Sunday is the bike ride.
Structure:	Mass start - although times are put on certificates.
Limit:	10,000.
Cost:	$15.00. Includes aid stations every 6.2 miles, awards, and fiesta at the end.

Promoter's Comments:
From the very beginning, I've worked with the State of Baja California, the cities, and convention bureaus of the towns involved to promote tourism to Baja. As an introduction to Baja, we organize a series of sporting events to provide something for everyone.

David Manwaring

RIDE NO. 5 - BAJA CALIFORNIA THREE CITIES RIDE

Contact: David Manwaring
                    Monday International, Inc.
                    P.O. Box 99120
                    San Diego, CA 92109
                    (619) 275-1384.

Year Began: Inaugural ride 1988.

The Ride: Following Manwaring's philosophy of something for everyone, all riders will start from Tijuana and pass through Rosarito Beach.   The first finish line is at 30 miles (Half Way House).   Those continuing on will finish at 67 miles in Ensenada.

Structure: Mass start.

Limit: Currently none.

Cost: $15.00.   Includes aid stations, awards and fiesta at end.

Promoter's Comments:
This is a new ride added to the series of fun-rides in Baja to promote tourism and introduce cyclists to riding in Baja.

David Manwaring

Tours

Aside from the Fun-Rides of Baja, there are several tour operators offering a wide variety of tours within Baja. There is even a non-profit, club-sponsored ride held annually that has become popular among touring cyclists looking for a challenge.

ANNUAL TOUR NO. 1 - THE KNICKERBIKERS CHRISTMAS ADVENTURE

Contact: Bob Wagner (leader)
                      12430 Royal Road
                      El Cajon, CA 92021
                      (619) 443-2532.

Year Began: 1975.

Annual Dates: 17 - 20 days of December, usually includes Christmas to New Year's Day.

The Trip: Tecate to Cabo San Lucas - 17 days and 1,065 miles. 1986 started the option of returning to La Paz adding 110 miles and 3 days.

Structure: A self-contained tour with camping and hotels. Each person takes care of his own meals. Sag support is not provided and is not welcomed.

Cost: $240.00 in 1986. Covers hotels and campgrounds, organization.

Comments:
This was a challenge ride when I started at age 39, and as I approach 51, it still is. It is not just a ride; it is an experience that's emotional and intense.

                                              Bob Wagner

ANNUAL TOUR NO. 2 - BAJA BICYCLE TOURS

Contact:	Bonnie Wong Touring Exchange, Inc. P.O. Box 265 Port Townsend, WA 98368 (206) 385-0667
Year Began:	1973.
Annual Dates:	Various tours conducted from November through April.
The Trips:	The schedule changes yearly with a wide variety of tours offered. There are 1 to 3 week paved road tours ranging from challenging 70 - 90 miles per day, to leisurely 35 - 40 miles per day. Most of these tours include an equipment vehicle and all meals. The schedule also includes dirt road, wilderness, mountain bike tours into the backcountry. Some are done on a self-contained basis and some are full-catered.
Limit:	Group sizes range from 6 - 12 per group.
Structure:	Paved road tours combine camping and hotels while the mountain bike tours are mostly all camping.
Cost:	Varies greatly depending on what services are provided with each tour. Send for current schedule and rates.

Comments:
Baja captured my spirit of adventure travel during a trip in 1973. I've returned eagerly every winter since, accompanied by fellow cyclists seeking a good bike ride, unusual scenery and a foreign culture. The 6 - 9 weeks in Baja are part of my winter survival program.

Bonnie Wong

APPENDIX NO. 6

Information Addresses

Mexican National Tourist Offices - West Coast

700 W. Georgia St.
Vancouver, British Columbia
Canada V7Y 1B6
(604) 682-0551

50 California St. #2465
San Francisco, CA 94111
(415) 986-0992

9701 Wilshire Blvd. #1201
Los Angeles, CA 90212
(213) 274-6315

Mexican Consulate
1333 Front St.
San Diego, CA 92101
(619) 231-8414

5151 E. Broadway
Tucson, AZ 85711
(602) 745-5055

Mexican Consulates - West Coast

The following are Mexican Consulate Addresses in west coast cities other than those which have Tourist Offices (as listed above)

1402 Third Ave., #720
Seattle, WA 98101
(206) 385-0667

809 Eighth St.
Sacramento, CA 95814
(916) 446-4696

380 North First
San Jose, CA 95112
(408) 294-3414

211 Tulare St.
Fresno, CA 93721
(209) 233-8714

Imperial Ave and 7th.
Calexico, CA 92231
(619) 357-3863

Baja Information Service

Baja Hotline - (800) 522-1516

Baja State Department of Tourism
P.O. Box 2448
Chula Vista, CA 92012

The telephone numbers of the various Baja State Tourism Offices are:

(706) 681-9492, 9493, or 9494 (in Tijuana)
(706) 654-1095 Tecate
(706) 676-2222 Ensenada
(706) 552-4391 Mexicali
(706) 577-1155 San Felipe

APPENDIX NO. 7

Bibliography, Selected Baja Publications and Maps

Books
There are numerous books on the market about Baja. Many of the guidebooks of the 1970s are outdated and are being replaced by more current editions. Many books are adventure stories of various people's travels throughout the peninsula. The following are suggested for their information and/or spirit of travel in Baja.

Baja Adventure Book by Walt Peterson, **Wilderness Press, Berkeley, CA 1987.**
This book took years of preparation and apparently left no stone unturned. Details on how-to and where-to for every sport and Baja type adventure are covered including diving, fishing, bicycling, backpacking, sea kayaking, cave exploring and much more.

Baja California - **Automobile Club of Southern California.**
Updated yearly. This book gives details on facilities throughout Baja and includes several dirt road excursions. Accompanying the book are separate listings of campgrounds and hotels on the peninsula and an excellent map. Available to members only. Can be ordered through your local AAA office.

Baja California and the Geography of Hope by Joseph Wood Krutch with Photographs by Eliot Porter, Sierra Club Press, San Francisco, CA 1967
This work is timeless. It is not a guidebook except, perhaps, in its philosophical treatment of the wonders of a desert wilderness. The photographs alone are excellent. Paperback or hardback.

Baja Lovers - by Bonnie Wong and illustrated by Kathleen Steffen. 1980. Touring Exchange, P.O. Box 265, Port Townsend, WA 98368.

This small volume is an anthology edited by Bonnie Wong. It contains stories and poems written by twelve bicyclists who have toured Baja. Revealing information, humorous episodes and unexpected encounters are told by those who have been there.

The Cave Paintings of Baja California - by Harry Crosby. Revised 1984. Sunbelt Publications, Box 191126, San Diego, CA 92119.

A large format, expensive, beautiful book. If you are truly interested in the ancient rock art found throughout the peninsula, this is the definitive book. Many color photos. Copley Books of La Jolla commissioned this work.

Field Guide to the Plants of Baja California by Jeanette Coyle and Norman Roberts. 1975. Natural History Publishing Co., Box 962, La Jolla, CA 92037.

An excellent guide to the cacti and plants of Baja, with extensive pen drawings and color photos. Paperback or hardback.

The Forgotten Peninsula - by Joseph Wood Krutch. Sierra Club Press, San Francisco, CA. Reprinted 1986.

This well-known desert naturalist writes of his journeys into Baja during the 1950s. Many of the questions regarding development and the terms of progress are even more valid today.

Keep it Moving, Baja by Canoe - by Valerie Fons. 1986. The Mountaineers, 306 Second Ave. West, Seattle, WA 98119.

It took 3.5 months to paddle the 2,411 miles of Baja's coastline. This is a tale of a two-person, adventure journey and of the author's resulting personal growth.

World of the California Gray Whale - by Tom Miller. 1975. Baja Trail Publications, Box 6088, Huntington Beach, CA 92615.
California residents add sales tax. If your Baja trip includes whale watching, this concise book will clue you in. Includes the history of whales and the whaling industry, the plight and comeback of the grays, and identification of California coastal, and other whales.

MAPS

Baja Topographic Atlas Directory 1986. Topography International, Inc., P.O. Box 5794, San Clemente, CA 92676-8794. Available from Touring Exchange, P.O. Box 265, Port Townsend, WA 98368.
Attention, Mountain Bikers! Over 200 large detailed maps covering all of Baja! Shows roads, trails, major route mileages, elevations, all principal cities, minor towns and villages, islands and much more. Includes directories of campgrounds, hotels, medical services, banks, and even has a comprehensive Spanish-English dictionary. For any backcountry touring, this detailed source is essential. Though expensive, this volume places the topographic maps of the entire peninsula, together with necessary touring information, in one binding. This is a real advantage when it comes to deciding which individual topo maps and which tour books should be carried on your tour. The book quickly pays for itself.

San Diego Regional Bicycling Map, Commuter Computer, P.O. Box 82358, San Diego, CA 92138.
Shows two-color designated bike routes in the San Diego area. Area covered extends to the border. However, this part of the map has been reproduced at a reduced scale and is very difficult to read.

Sources

Map Centre, Inc. - **2611** University Ave., San Diego, CA 92104-2894, (619) 291-3830
This book and map store carries topographic maps including Baja and mainland Mexico.

Sunbelt Publications, P.O. Box 191126, San Diego, CA 92119
Sunbelt is a distributor and publisher of an extensive number of books, maps and other publications on Baja and the U.S. Southwest. A list of available publications will be sent on SASE request.

Index

Author Bonnie Wong

Author/photographer Bonnie Wong has been conducting bicycle tours throughout the Baja Peninsula since 1973. She also has conducted biking tours throughout North America and as far away as New Zealand. Bonnie now lives in Port Townsend, Washington, where TOURING EXCHANGE, her adventure/travel business, co-habits a store with P. T. Cyclery. With over thirty magazine articles and two books to her credit, Bonnie currently conducts cycle-tours of the great Pacific Northwest each summer and the magical Baja peninsula each winter - a compelling version of the best of two worlds.

OTHER BIKING & BAJA BOOKS

Available at better book stores and bike shops in Southern California or from:

SUNBELT PUBLICATIONS
POB 191126
SAN DIEGO, CA 92119-1126
(619) 448-0884

Sunbelt Publications is the largest bicycle book and the leading Baja book distributor on the West Coast. Call or write for free catalog. All prices subject to change. California residents add 6% sales tax. Add $2.00 for postage and handling.

BICYCLE BOOKS

ANZA-BORREGO DESERT REGION
by Lowell and Diana Lindsay. 2nd edition 1986. The best selling and most authoritative guide to Southern California's largest desert preserve, a popular area for mountain biking and road touring. $10.95.

BICYCLING BAJA
by Bonnie Wong. 1988. The guide by Baja's premier bike tour operator based on years of experience over thousands of miles of paved and off-road routes. $12.95.

BICYCLING THE PACIFIC COAST
by Tom and Vicky Kirkendall. 1984. Details the 1,947 mile Pacific Coast bike route from Canada to Mexico. Route is in 50 mile segments. $9.95

BICYCLE TOURING IN THE WESTERN UNITED STATES
by Karen and Gary Hawkins. 1982. Details 23 tours, three in the Southwest. Tour linked end to end to provide several attractive cross country routes. $9.95.

BICYCLIST'S EMERGENCY REPAIR
by Don Alexander. Covers the required tools and procedures (with step-by-step photo illustrations). $5.95.

BIKE BAG BOOK
by Tom Cuthbertson and Rick Morrall. A well-written manual for emergency roadside bicycle repair. $2.95.

BIKE TOURS IN SOUTHERN ARIZONA
by Ed Stiles and Mort Solot. 1980. Describes various tours in the Phoenix and Tucson areas and includes 20 maps. $5.95.

CALIFORNIA COAST BICYCLE ROUTE
by Bikecentennial. 1987. Map books that contain descriptions of the popular 1000-mile coastal route. In 3 sections: (1) Crescent City to San Francisco - 325 miles, (2) San Francisco to Santa Barbara - 375 miles, (3) Santa Barbara to San Diego - 250 miles. Each section $6.95.

CYCLING SAN DIEGO
by Jerry Schad and Don Krupp. 1986. Provides detailed descriptions of 36 trips throughout the city of San Diego and San Diego County. Includes parks, shoreline areas, and back-country tours. $8.95.

GRAND CANYON TO MEXICO BICYCLE ROUTE
by Ed and Lori Stiles. 1982. Bike-pack guidebook reduces route to 5 well described segments. Includes maps, elevation profiles, camps and other details. $4.95.

GREAT PARKS SOUTH EXTENSION
by Bikecentennial. Description of 370-mile extension of Great Parks Bicycle Route linking Colorado with Southwest America Bicycle Route. $3.95.

LONE STAR BICYCLE ROUTE
by John Gaynor and Texas Cycling. 1976. A folded map of Lone Star Route from Amarillo to Bon Wier, Texas. Includes cumulative miles, public camps, and climatic information. $3.00.

SOUTHERN OVERLAND ROUTE
by Lowell and Diana Lindsay. 1985.

Detailed description of cross country route emphasizing fascinating historic and scenic features along pioneer trails through the Southwest. Includes 17 maps, one is the connecting Lone Star Route between Amarillo and Bon Wier, Texas. $7.95.

SOUTHWEST AMERICA BICYCLE ROUTE
by Lowell Lindsay and W. G. Hample. 1987. Description of popular cross country route connecting Southern California with TransAmerica Route in Larned, Kansas. Route divided into 26 tours. Each includes route, camps, points of interest. $9.95.

BOOKS ON BAJA CALIFORNIA

BAJA BOOK III
by Tom Miller. 1987. Latest edition of most popular and best selling guide to the peninsula by one of Baja's best known travel writers. $11.95.

BAJA ROAD LOG
by Walt Wheelock. 1987. Numerous highway and off-pavement routes with detailed logs. Bike bag size. $6.95.

BAJA TOPOGRAPHIC ATLAS
by Landon Crumpton. 1987. The most detailed compendium of maps available plus much additional information. $24.95.

BEACHES OF BAJA
by Walt Wheelock. 1985. The perennially popular guide to Baja's strands from San Quintin and San Felipe north. $3.50.

BORDER TOWNS OF THE SOUTHWEST.
by Rick Cahill. 1987. Interesting and valuable information for the traveler about Tijuana, Tecate, and Mexicali. $9.95.

CABO SAN LUCAS
by Susan Crow. 1984. Detailed guide to the fascinating "land's end" region of the 1000 mile peninsula. $8.95.

CAMPING AND CLIMBING IN BAJA
by John Robinson. 1983. Useful for the mountain bike explorer in bike bag size. Maps and photos of Northern Baja. $4.50.

CANON DE LOS ARTISTAS
by Austin Deuel. 1986. Superb photos and paintings of the most fascinating and mysterious archaeological area of Baja. Protected as a national and human treasure, some sites are yet accessible to the discreet explorer. $35.00.

CAVE PAINTINGS OF BAJA
by Harry Crosby. 1984. Detailed pictures and narrative of this midriff mountain stronghold where the hills sing and the rocks speak with the forgotten tongues of the ancient ones. $27.50.

EATING YOUR WAY THROUGH BAJA
by Tom Miller. 1986. A fun guide to the culinary side of the Baja experience. $4.95.

HOLA TIJUANA
by Susan Eichhorn. 1987. Where-to and what-to in the second largest metropolis on the West Coast of North America and the world's most popular border corssing. Highlights of superb new shopping malls, museums and art galleries, plus luxury hotel and dining attractions. $4.95.

MAGNIFICENT PENINSULA
by Jack Williams. 1987. Comprehensive guide to all of Baja with particular emphasis on the lore and lure of her natural and human history. Essential to understanding this magic land. $14.95.

PEOPLES GUIDE TO MEXICO
by Carl Franz. 1986. The classic and highly acclaimed work for the adventure traveler in our most populous neighbor land with emphasis on coping with the real encounters of foreign culture, custom, and language. Describes the land and people beyond the glitzy facade of tourist brochure. $13.95.

ORDER FORM

To: SUNBELT PUBLICATIONS
      P.O. BOX 191126
      SAN DIEGO, CA 92119-1126

I am enclosing $_____ which includes shipping and handling fees
and California State Sales Tax (if applicable), for the following books:

BICYCLE BOOKS

( )   Anza-Borrego Desert Region @ $10.95
( )   Bicycling Baja @ $12.95
( )   Bicycling the Pacific Coast @ $9.95
( )   Bicycle Touring in the Western United States @ $9.95
( )   Bicyclist's Emergency Repair @ $5.95
( )   Bike Bag Book @ $2.95
( )   Bike Tours in Southern Arizona @ $5.95
( )   California Coast Bicycle Route, Crescent City to San Francisco
      @ $6.95
( )   California Coast Bicycle Route, San Francisco to Santa Barbara
      @ $6.95
( )   California Coast Bicycle Route, Santa Barbara to San Diego
      @ $6.95
( )   Cycling San Diego @ $8.95
( )   Grand Canyon to Mexico Bicycle Route @ $4.95
( )   Great Parks South Extension @ $3.95
( )   Lone Star Bicycle Route @ $3.00
( )   Southern Overland Route @ $7.95
( )   Southwest America Bicycle Route @ $9.95

Total $_____ Please include $2.00 shipping and handling fees
and add 6% sales tax for books shipped to California addresses.

Your name_____

Address_____

City_____State_____ZIP_____

ORDER FORM

To: SUNBELT PUBLICATIONS
       P.O. BOX 191126
       SAN DIEGO, CA 92119-1126

I am enclosing $_____ which includes shipping and handling fees
and California State Sales Tax (if applicable), for the following books:

BAJA BOOKS

( )   Baja Book III @ $11.95
( )   Baja Road Log @ $6.95
( )   Baja Topographic Atlas @ $24.95
( )   Beaches of Baja @ $3.50
( )   Border Towns of the Southwest @ $9.95
( )   Cabo San Lucas @ $8.95
( )   Camping and Climbing in Baja @ $4.50
( )   Canon De Los Artistas @ $35.00
( )   Cave Paintings of Baja @ $27.50
( )   Eating Your Way Through Baja @ $4.95
( )   Hola Tijuana @ $4.95
( )   Magnificent Peninsula @ $14.95
( )   Peoples Guide to Mexico @ $13.95

Total $_____ Please include $2.00 shipping and handling fees
and add 6% sales tax for books shipped to California addresses.

Your name_____

Address_____

City_____State_____ZIP_____